KU-617-378

REWARD

Item Number

13704

REWARD

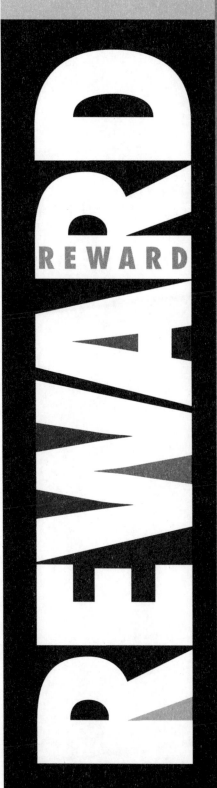

Pre-intermediate

Business Resource Pack

Communicative activities for students of Business English

Colin Benn
Paul Dummett

MACMILLAN
HEINEMANN
English Language Teaching

Macmillan Heinemann English Language Teaching
Between Towns Road, Oxford OX4 3PP

A division of Macmillan Publishers Limited

Companies and representatives throughout the world

ISBN 0 435 240366

Text © Colin Benn and Paul Dummett 1995
Design and illustration © Macmillan Publishers 1998
First published 1995

Permission to copy

The material in this book is copyright. However, the publisher grants
permission for copies of pages to be made without fee on those pages
marked with the PHOTOCOPIABLE symbol.

Private purchasers may make copies for their own use or for use by
classes of which they are in charge; school purchasers may make
copies for use within and by the staff and students of the school only.
This permission does not extend to additional schools or branches of
an institution, who should purchase a separate master copy of the
book for their own use.

For copying in any other circumstances, prior permission in writing
must be obtained from Macmillan Publishers Limited.

Designed by D & J Hunter
Cover design by Stafford & Stafford
Illustrations by
Nancy Anderson, Kathy Baxendale, Peter Bull, Joan Corlass, Keith Cowlan,
David Downton, Gillian Martin, Ed McLachlan, Peter Schrank, Gary Wing

Authors' acknowledgements
The authors would like to thank Catherine Smith and Angela Reckitt at
Macmillan Publishers and Michelle Zahran and the staff at Regent Oxford
for their help with the Business Resource Pack.

Printed and bound in Great Britain by Martins the Printers Ltd.,
Berwick-upon-Tweed

2003   2002   2001   2000
11   10   9   8   7   6   5

Contents

Worksheet	Interaction	Skills	Activity	Time (Mins)	Grammar and functions	Business Vocabulary
20 *How long does it take?*	Pairwork	Speaking	Information gap: asking about time, distance and cost on a business trip	30	Question forms with *how, what,* and *kind of*	Travel
Progress check 16–20 *Crossword*	Pairwork	Reading Speaking	Crossword: revising financial vocabulary	30	Revision	Money Methods of payment
21a and 21b *Choosing the right candidate* 21a Recruitment details 21b CVs	Pairwork	Reading Speaking Writing	Job interviews: discussing education, qualifications and experience; writing a memo	30	Present perfect simple Past simple Talking about experience	Job advertisements The environment
22a *Government measures*	Pairwork	Speaking Writing	Communication task: discussing recent actions and results Writing a report	25	Present perfect simple for past actions with present results	The economy
22b *Problem solving*	Pairwork	Speaking Writing	Discussing solutions to company problems; reporting on action taken Writing a memo	25	Present perfect simple for describing recent actions	Hotels
23 *Business history*	Pairwork	Speaking	Talking about business and political events	15	Present perfect simple with *for* and *since*	General Noun phrases
24 *What's the word for … ?*	Pairwork	Speaking	Game: giving definitions of words and guessing their meanings	40	Defining relative clauses using *who, which* and *where*	Company terms
25 *Patent pending*	Groupwork	Speaking	Mill drill: describing objects and their function	25	Talking about function and purpose	Gadgets
Progress check 21–25 *Success story*	Pairwork Whole class	Reading Speaking Writing	Communication task: talking about someone's career and achievements Writing a paragraph describing someone's achievements	30	Present perfect Past simple	Computing General
26 *The right qualifications*	Pairwork	Speaking	Job advertisements Deciding on the right qualifications for a job	25	Obligation, necessity and lack of necessity: *must, don't have to, don't need to*	Qualifications and skills
27 *In answer to your letter*	Pairwork	Writing	Writing a business letter Answering an enquiry	35	*Can* for ability The conventions of letter writing	General
28 *What are the rules?*	Pairwork	Speaking	Discussing advertising standards in different countries	30	*Can* and *can't* for permission and prohibition	Trading Advertising
29 *Communication skills*	Groupwork	Speaking	Discussing how to give a presentation, chair a meeting, write a report	30	*Should* and *shouldn't* for advice and recommendation	Time expressions Communication skills
30a and 30b *Everyday requests* 30a Game board 30b Cards	Groupwork	Speaking Writing	Board game: making everyday requests while travelling Writing a letter	30	Requests Asking for permission	Travel
Progress check 26–30 *Business terms*	Groupwork	Speaking	Discussion Vocabulary matching and extension	30	Common adjective and noun collocations	Business terms
31 *Health and safety*	Groupwork	Reading Speaking	Communication task: describing accidents at work; making recommendations	30	Past continuous, past simple *Should* for recommendations	Health and safety
32 *The conditions for change*	Pairwork	Reading Speaking	Speaking about the background to important events	30	Past continuous for describing background events	General
33 *A problem with a supplier*	Pairwork	Reading Writing	Writing and exchanging faxes between customer and supplier	30	*Too* + adjective; *not* + adjective + *enough*	Trade
34 *A manufacturing process*	Groupwork	Speaking	Problem solving; describing a manufacturing process Deciding on the layout of a factory	30	Present simple passive Sequencing: *too* + adjective *Must*	Production
35 *Entertaining a client*	Pairwork	Speaking Writing	Role play: explaining the dishes on a menu to a business guest Writing a thank-you letter	30	Revision of present simple passive Suggestions and recommendations	Food, cooking and taste
Progress check 31–35 *Phrasal verbs*	Pairwork Groupwork	Speaking	Mill drill or card game to practise business phrasal verbs	30	Revision of *Yes/No* questions Mixed tenses	Phrasal verbs
36 *Business news*	Pairwork	Speaking	Reading and discussing business news headlines Writing a news story	30	*Might* for future possibility Speculating about the future	Business news General
37 *Discussing options*	Groupwork Pairwork	Reading Speaking Writing	Discussing company options and deciding on a course of action Writing a memo	40	First conditional *Should* for advice	Mixed verbs
38 *What would you do?*	Pairwork	Speaking Writing	Questionnaire: problem solving	30	Second conditional	General
39 *Diplomacy*	Groupwork	Speaking	Choosing polite and appropriate language Writing a letter	20	*Would* and *could* for polite requests	Negotiation
40 *Negotiation*	Pairwork	Speaking Writing	Arranging a meeting Negotiating a contract Writing a memo	40	Second conditional: *would* and *could* Making proposals Arranging a meeting	Negotiation Tennis
Progress check 36–40 *An informal meeting*	Groupwork	Speaking Writing	Meeting to discuss ways of motivating a sales team Writing a report	25	First and second conditionals	Incentives

Questions	Company 1 Name _____	Company 2 Name _____	Company 3 Name _____
What do people usually wear to work?			
How do people greet each other?			
Do people use first names?			
Where do people eat during the working week?			
What social activities do employees do together outside work?			
Do men and women have different roles in the company?			
What training does the company give to its employees?			
What benefits do people get from the company? (not their salaries)			
How long do people usually stay with the company?			
How often do people move from one department to another?			
What age do people retire at?			

© Macmillan Publishers Limited 1995.

Company culture **Worksheet** *1a*

NOTE: This activity is not linked to the activity on Worksheet 1b.

ACTIVITY
Pairwork: speaking, writing

AIM
To find out about working practices in different companies/countries.

GRAMMAR AND FUNCTIONS
Present simple: questions with and without question words
Adverbs of frequency: *usually, often*
Asking for and giving information

VOCABULARY
Working practices and behaviour: *greet, employee, retire, benefits, training*

PREPARATION
Make a copy of the worksheet for each student.

TIME
30 to 40 minutes

PROCEDURE
1   Go through the questions on the worksheet with the class, asking students to suggest possible answers for each question. Don't make reference yet to any specific company or country. For example, for the first question, *casual clothes, uniform, a suit,* etc; for the second question, *shake hands, bow, 'hello'* etc.

2   Ask students to write down on their worksheet the answers for their own company or a company they know well.

3   In pairs, students now ask about each other's companies and write down the information on their worksheets. They can repeat this two or three times with different partners. In a class discussion ask the students to report back on what they have discovered, particularly anything which they found unusual or surprising.

FOLLOW-UP
Ask the students to write a short letter to a friend describing working practices in a company, beginning like this:
Dear Colin,
You asked me for some information about Revulux and Co. I know that people in this company usually use first names and...

© Macmillan Publishers Limited 1995.

CIT

Daniel Carne
DIRECTOR

Council on International Training
33 Seymour Place
London W1H 6AS

NURIA MARTINEZ
Production Manager

Intex Plastics SA

Plaza Segovia, Madrid 101010
Tel: 1 324 5 472 Fax: 1 324 6 880

Elizabeth Richelieu
Research Scientist
(Plastics division)

Rue de Londres
75009 Paris
Tel: 40 45 60 87 – Fax: 40 53 88 88

Alchem
FRANCE

R&R

Nelson da Silva
Financial Consultant

Reubens and Reubens
Rua de São Miguel, 18
Lisbon
Tel: 53 91 08
Fax: 35 11 66 15 96

Takeshi Toyama
Company Training Manager

Kanai Department Store

Ginza
Tokyo
Tel: 81 3 3400392

Penny Chiu
LECTURER

• School • of • Computer • Science •

The International University
TAIPEI
TAIWAN

Paul Paradan

AREA SALES MANAGER (MIDDLE EAST)
SFG Generators
Rue du 4 Septembre, Lausanne CH 20090

Kylie Taylor
Sales Representative
(Far East)

SILVER STUD SHIRT COMPANY

Forks Industrial Park
Melbourne 16
Australia   Tel: 61–3–72292

Kirsten Lofgrund
Financial Controller

Bioskan AG

Per Olafswag
Stockholm
Sweden
Tel: 46 8 63 145 27

Gerhard Reiner
Software Consultant

REINER SOLUTIONS

Heilbronnerstrasse, 17
Salzburg
AUSTRIA
Tel: 43-662-209 60

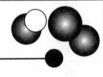

NAME	NATIONALITY	COMPANY NAME	JOB
	Swedish	*Bioskan AG*	
	French		*Research Scientist*
Gerhard Reiner			*Software Consultant*
Daniel Carne			
		Reubens and Reubens	
	Taiwanese		*Senior Lecturer*
		Silver Stud Shirt Co	
Takeshi Toyama	*Japanese*		
Nuria Martinez			
Paul Paradan		*SFG Generators*	

© Macmillan Publishers Limited 1995.

First meetings and introductions **Worksheet** **1b**

NOTE: This activity is not linked to the activity on Worksheet 1a.

ACTIVITY
Pairwork or groupwork: speaking

AIM
To introduce yourself and others.

GRAMMAR AND FUNCTIONS
Questions: *What…? Where…? Who…?*
Introductions: *My name is…/I'm…*
Greetings
Spellings

VOCABULARY
Company names and job titles: *financial consultant/controller, production manager, research scientist, lecturer, engineer, software consultant, director, training manager, sales representative*
The alphabet

PREPARATION
Cut the table off the bottom of the worksheet and make one copy of it for each student in the class. Make one copy of the cards for each group of up to ten students and cut them out as indicated.

TIME
20 minutes

PROCEDURE
1 Copy this business card onto the board.
> Sarah Cole
> Journalist
> The Daily News
> 74 Warwick Street
> Birmingham BJ2 8QT

Then model the activity, acting out a dialogue like this:
> A: *Hello, I'm Colin Benn.*
> B: *Pleased to meet you. I'm Sarah Cole.*
> A: *Are you English?*
> B: *Yes, I'm from Birmingham.*
> A: *Who do you work for?*
> B: *I'm a journalist for the Daily News.*
> A: *Oh, really? I work for a newspaper too.*

2 Ask the students to work in groups of between four and ten and give a business card and table to each student.

3 Explain that they have to complete the table by introducing themselves to one another. They also have to find someone who works in the same field or does the same job as they do.

4 Go through the answers with the whole class by asking students to introduce the person with whom they found something in common.

FOLLOW-UP
Ask the students to act out similar dialogues using their own names and company names.

ANSWERS

Name	Nationality	Company Name	Job
Kirsten Lofgrund	Swedish	Bioskan AG	Financial Controller
Elizabeth Richelieu	French	Alchem	Research Scientist
Gerhard Reiner	Austrian	Reiner Solutions	Software Consultant
Daniel Carne	British	CIT	Director
Nelson da Silva	Portuguese	Reubens and Reubens	Financial Consultant
Penny Chiu	Taiwanese	The International University	Senior Lecturer
Kylie Taylor	Australian	Silver Stud Shirt Co	Sales Representative
Takeshi Toyama	Japanese	Kanai Department Store	Company Training Manager
Nuria Martinez	Spanish	Intex Plastics SA	Production Manager
Paul Paradan	Swiss	SFG Generators	Area Sales Manager

© Macmillan Publishers Limited 1995.

Table

NAME	Kuni Hayashi	Katerina Schmidt	Chantal Guerlain	Firas Marwan	Carlos Lopes
COMPANY					
JOB					
TRANSPORT TO WORK					
TRAVEL TIME TO WORK					
WORKING HOURS					
TRAVEL ABROAD					

NOTES

1 _____
2 _____
3 _____
4 _____
5 _____
6 _____
7 _____
8 _____

© Macmillan Publishers Limited 1995.

PHOTOCOPIABLE

Work routines Worksheets 2a and 2b

NOTE: Use Worksheets 2a and 2b for this activity.

ACTIVITY
Groupwork: speaking

AIM
To find missing information by asking about the routines of five working people.

GRAMMAR AND FUNCTIONS
Present simple statements and questions (especially third person singular)
Adverbs of frequency
Talking about routines

VOCABULARY
Means of transport
Company and job titles

PREPARATION
Make one copy for each student of Worksheet 2a (table) and one copy of Worksheet 2b (sentences) for every group of six students in the class. Cut out the sentences into six cards as indicated.

TIME
25 minutes

PROCEDURE
1 Give the table to each student and elicit the correct question from each prompt. For example,
> Job: *What does Kuni Hayashi do?*
> Travel time to work: *How long does it take Chantal Guerlain to get to work?* etc

2 Ask the students to work in groups of three or six. Give a different card or pair of cards to each student in the group.

3 Ask the students to read their sentences and write in the table any definite information they now have and to write in the notes section information which they cannot yet place on the table.

4 Ask students to mix with the other students in their group and ask each other questions in order to complete the table. Tell them to do it as quickly as they can but not to show their tables or sentences to the other members of the group. (It could be a race between groups if you wish.)

5 When they have finished, go through the answers by asking students to give a profile of each person. For example:
Kuni Hayashi is a salesman. He works for Manebo Cosmetics. He goes to work by train and it usually takes him...

PAIRWORK OPTION
Do the activity in the way described above, but ask the students to work in pairs, giving each student three cards. Allow extra time for the students to read and transfer their information in step 3.

© Macmillan Publishers Limited 1995.

Sentences

The salesman works for Manebo Cosmetics.

Katerina Schmidt doesn't travel abroad often.

Chantal Guerlain goes to work by car and sometimes by helicopter.

Firas Marwan works 4 nights a week.

The bank manager travels to work by car.

The woman who drives a motorbike is an engineer.

Carlos Lopes is a bank manager.

The managing director travels abroad very often (every week).

Kuni Hayashi's train journey takes 2 hours.

Firas Marwan usually walks to work.

It takes Carlos Lopes 30 minutes to get to work.

Firas Marwan never travels abroad in his job.

Kuni Hayashi usually works 50–55 hours a week.

The managing director usually works 7 days a week.

The engineer works for Keiler Electronics.

Chantal Guerlain works for Mann's Hotel Group.

The walk to the hospital takes 20 minutes.

The salesman goes to work by train.

The bank manager works for the Housing Bank of Brazil.

It takes Katerina Schmidt 5 minutes to get to work.

Carlos Lopes works 30 hours a week.

Katerina Schmidt goes to work by motorbike.

It takes 20 minutes to fly to the hotel's head office.

Kuni Hayashi often travels abroad (three times a month).

The night worker is a nurse.

Engineers at Keiler Electronics work between 37 and 40 hours a week.

Chantal Guerlain is a managing director.

Carlos Lopes sometimes travels to Buenos Aires.

The nurse works at the Al-Hijazi hospital.

Kuni Hayashi works for Manebo Cosmetics.

© Macmillan Publishers Limited 1995.

PHOTOCOPIABLE

Work routines Worksheet 2b

ANSWERS

NAME	Kuni Hayashi	Katerina Schmidt	Chantal Guerlain	Firas Marwan	Carlos Lopes
COMPANY	Manebo Cosmetics	Keiler Electronics	Mann's Hotel Group	Al-Hijazi hospital	Housing Bank of Brazil
JOB	salesman	engineer	managing director	nurse	bank manager
TRANSPORT TO WORK	train	motorbike	car and sometimes helicopter	on foot	car
TRAVEL TIME TO WORK	2 hours	5 minutes	20 minutes	20 minutes	30 minutes
WORKING HOURS	50–55 hours a week	37–40 hours a week	7 days a week	4 nights a week	30 hours
TRAVEL ABROAD	often travels abroad	not often	every week	no	sometimes to Buenos Aires

© Macmillan Publishers Limited 1995.

Company profile

Company name	Astra Lamps UK Ltd
Type of company	Lighting equipment importer and supplier
Number of employees	430
Headquarters	Astra Lamps International, Nijmegen, Netherlands
Comments	The company is looking for a good place to set up a sales office and warehouse to supply the British market. There are two possibilities: one in Kingston and one at Fordham, about 20 kilometers from Kingston.

THE BUILDING

Location	
Size of main building	
Number of offices	
Warehouse	
Car park	
Other facilities	

THE AREA

Transport	
Bus	
Trains	
Housing	
Schools	
Shops	

© Macmillan Publishers Limited 1995.

PHOTOCOPIABLE

Is there a warehouse? Worksheets **3a** and **3b**

NOTE: Use Worksheets 3a and 3b for this activity.

ACTIVITY
Pairwork: speaking

AIM
To choose a new building for your company by talking about the facilities offered at two sites.

GRAMMAR AND FUNCTIONS
There is/there are, have/have got
Statement and question forms
Describing business premises

VOCABULARY
Buildings: *warehouse, factory, office, car park, canteen, reception*

PREPARATION
Make one copy of Worksheet 3a for each student, and one copy of Worksheet 3b (map) for every other student. Cut out pictures A and B as indicated.

TIME
25 minutes

PROCEDURE
1 Elicit from the students the names of the different buildings and parts of a company. For example: *office, factory, warehouse, canteen.*

2 Give a copy of Worksheet 3a to each student and ask them to read the Company Profile.

3 Ask the students to read the checklist under the headings, 'The Building' and 'The Area' and elicit the appropriate questions.
For example:
　Location: *Where is the building?*
　Warehouse: *Has it got a warehouse? How big is it?*
　Trains: *Is there a railway station near the factory?*

4 Ask students to work in pairs and divide them into Student A and Student B. Give each Student A a copy of map A and each Student B a copy of map B. Give them a few minutes to study the sites.

5 Ask students to ask and answer questions about the building and area in their partner's picture. They should note down the answers on the worksheet.

6 When they have finished, the students should, together, decide which of the two sites is the more suitable or attractive.

7 Ask students to report back their decision to the rest of the class, giving their reasons.

FOLLOW-UP
Ask students to write a memorandum to their Managing Director, recommending the site they have chosen.
Begin like this:
Site for new factory
We looked at the two buildings yesterday and we recommend the _____. It has got _____ and there is...

© Macmillan Publishers Limited 1995.

Maps

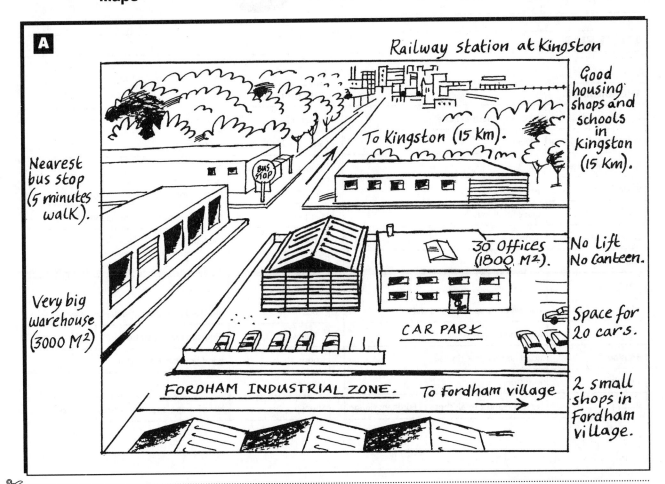

A

Railway station at Kingston

To Kingston (15 km).

Good housing shops and schools in Kingston (15 km).

Nearest bus stop (5 minutes walk).

Very big warehouse (3000 M²)

30 Offices (1800 M²).

No lift No Canteen.

CAR PARK

Space for 20 cars.

FORDHAM INDUSTRIAL ZONE.

To Fordham village →

2 small shops in Fordham village.

B

Kingston has a railway station, a lot of good shops, a sports centre and 2 cinemas.

Bus stops in market street and High street.

Lots of houses in Kingston and 2 schools.

HIGH STREET

60 offices (3000 M²)

MARKET STREET

KINGSTON TOWN CENTRE

Warehouse space in Newton is large. (6000 square metres).

No canteen small lift.

Small car park at back.

No warehouse in Kingston (Nearest warehouse 5 Km outside the town — see photograph).

© Macmillan Publishers Limited 1995.

PHOTOCOPIABLE

Is there a warehouse? **Worksheet** *3b*

ANSWERS

A

THE BUILDING	
Location	Fordham Industrial Zone
Size of main building	1800m^2
Number of offices	30
Warehouse	yes
Car park	space for 20 cars
Other facilities	none
THE AREA	
Transport:	
Bus	nearest bus stop 5 minutes walk
Trains	Kingston railway station – 15km
Housing	good housing in Kingston
Schools	Kingston
Shops	Kingston and 2 small shops in Fordham village

B

THE BUILDING	
Location	Kingston
Size of main building	3000m^2
Number of offices	60
Warehouse	nearest warehouse 5 km outside town
Car park	small car park at back of building
Other facilities	small lift
THE AREA	
Transport:	
Bus	bus stops in Market Street/High Street
Trains	Kingston railway station
Housing	good housing in Kingston
Schools	2
Shops	lots of shops, a sports centre, 2 cinemas

© Macmillan Publishers Limited 1995.

DO YOU LIKE...?	YES	NO	DON'T MIND
being part of a team			
managing people			
working with figures			
working under pressure			
helping people			
buying and selling things			
working in an office			
socializing			
working on a computer			
physical exercise			
travelling			
ARE YOU GOOD AT...?	**YES**	**NO**	**NOT BAD**
taking decisions			
solving problems			
organizing			
making things			
thinking of new ideas			
explaining things to people			
communicating your ideas			

--- fold --

International Red Cross aid worker

Door-to-door salesman (vacuum cleaners)

Wall Street stock exchange dealer

Advertising executive

Editor – Business Magazine

Fire chief (local fire station)

Personal Assistant to the Managing Director of a large insurance company

Ski instructor

I think _____ would be a good _____

because he/she likes _____ and he/she is good at _____

_____ . He/she is also good at _____ and this is very

important for a _____ .

© Macmillan Publishers Limited 1995.

Do you like working under pressure? **Worksheet** 4

ACTIVITY
Pairwork and groupwork: reading and speaking

AIM
To speak about work skills and preferences and choose suitable jobs.

GRAMMAR AND FUNCTIONS
Verbs with the gerund: *like/don't like + -ing, be good at + -ing*
Talking about likes and abilities

VOCABULARY
Work skills and functions: *to manage people, to solve problems, to take decisions, to think of (new ideas), to work with figures, to explain something to someone, to be part of a team*
Specific job titles

PREPARATION
Make a copy of the worksheet for each student in the class and fold the worksheet where indicated.

TIME
30 to 40 minutes

PROCEDURE
1   Elicit some of the vocabulary by asking the students what qualities are needed for a) a secretary and b) an office manager. Write some of the suggestions on the board.

2   Give a copy of the questionnaire to each student and ask them to read it but not to fill it in.

3   Ask the students to work in pairs. In turn, they ask each other the questions on the questionnaire and fill in their partner's answers.

4   When they have completed the table, each student should summarise their partner's skills and preferences and advise them what type of work would suit them best.

5   Ask each pair of students to join other pairs to make a group of six to eight students.

6   In their groups, ask the students to unfold their worksheets and discuss the jobs on offer on the noticeboard and say which skills are needed for each job.

7   When they have done this, ask each student to look at the previously completed questionnaire and propose a job for their partner, giving reasons for their choice.

8   Ask the students to write this information down by completing the paragraph at the bottom of the worksheet.

9   Conduct a class discussion on the job each student has chosen for their partner. Is their partner happy? If not, why not?

© Macmillan Publishers Limited 1995.

KEY	**Syntax Engineering**
Reception/Showroom	Receive customers, answer calls. A: Tamara, the receptionist/talk/to our sales manager.
Sales office	Take orders for new parts. B, C, D: The sales staff/have/a meeting (do not disturb!)
Design office	Engineers make drawings by hand or on computer. E: Margaret, the Chief Engineer/design/a new water pump.
Workshop	Machine operators make parts. F: Karl, the production foreman/explain/the production plan to the workers.
Stores	Store materials; send finished parts to customers. G: Anna, the stores manager/check/the stock.

Tildemann's Bank   **Syntax Engineering**

Showing someone around

NOTE: Use Worksheets 5a and 5b for this activity.

ACTIVITY
Pairwork: speaking

AIM
To give a guided tour of a company and describe the work in different departments.

GRAMMAR AND FUNCTIONS
Present simple contrasted with present continuous
Demonstrative pronouns: *this, that*

VOCABULARY
Departments and parts of a building
Verbs of communication: *advise, explain*

PREPARATION
Make copies of Worksheet 5a and Worksheet 5b and divide them equally among the class.

TIME
30 minutes

PROCEDURE
1   Elicit the names of the different sections/departments the students would expect to find in a bank and an engineering firm. For example, *reception, cashier's position, manager's office, workshop.*

2   Tell the students that they are going to show each other around a company. They must explain to their partner a) what happens in each department and b) what the people who work there are doing at the moment.

3   Demonstrate by drawing a plan of two or three rooms on the board and telling the class that this is a plan of part of the school.
    Point to the plan and say: *This is the reception area/teacher's room/director's office.* Encourage students to ask questions.
    For example:
    What happens here? Who works here?
    Give model answers and, if necessary, write them on the board.
    For example: *The teachers prepare their lessons. The director works here. She's telephoning an agent.*

4   Put students into pairs of one Student A and one Student B. Give each Student A a copy of Worksheet 5a and each Student B a copy of Worksheet 5b.

5   Ask the students to read the information in the Key at the top of the worksheet regarding the company. Explain that they are going to take it in turns to show each other around their company.

6   Ask the students to ask questions about their partner's company as they are being shown round. Point out the model sentences on the board if the students need more guidance.

7   When they have finished, ask one or two students from each group to tell you what they have found out. Do the other students agree with the information?

FOLLOW-UP
Ask the students to do the same activity using a plan of their own company offices or a part of the building you are in.

© Macmillan Publishers Limited 1995.

	Tildemann's Bank
KEY	
Main banking hall	Customers put in, take out money; exchange foreign currency. A: A customer/look/at her account on a computer.
Reception area	Staff answer customers' questions. B: Janet, a receptionist/give/information to customers.
Clearing area	Clear cheques. C: Technician/put in/a new computer system.
Loans department	Assistant manager arranges loans for customers. F: Assistant manager/discuss/loan/on the telephone.
Investments department	Staff advise customers on the best way to invest their money. D & E: Sarah/look at/share prices with a customer.

Tildemann's Bank

Syntax Engineering

Showing someone around Worksheet 5b

POSSIBLE ANSWERS

SYNTAX ENGINEERING

A: is the reception area. The receptionist receives customers and answers the telephone. Tamara, the receptionist, is talking to our sales manager at the moment.

B, C, D: is the sales office. The sales staff take orders for new parts. At the moment they are having a meeting – do not disturb!

E: is the design office. This is where the engineers make drawings by hand or on computer. At the moment, Margaret, the chief engineer, is designing a new water pump.

F: is the workshop. The machine operators make parts here. Karl, the production foreman, is explaining the production plan to the workers.

G: is the stores. We store materials here before sending it to customers. Anna, the stores manager, is checking the stock.

TILDEMANN'S BANK

A: is the main banking hall. Customers pay in and take out money here. At the moment a customer is looking at her account on the computer.

B: is the reception area. This is where the staff answer questions. Janet, the receptionist, is giving some information to customers.

C: is the clearing area. This is where the cheques are cleared. The technicians are putting in a new computer system at the moment.

D, E: is the investments department. This is where the staff advise customers how to invest their money. At the moment Sarah is looking at share prices with a customer.

F: is the loans department. This is where the assistant manager arranges loans with customers. He is arranging a loan at the moment.

© Macmillan Publishers Limited 1995.

Royal Swedish Crystal

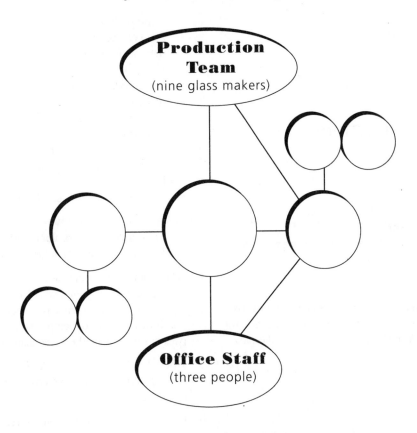

✂ ───

Suralex Glass Products

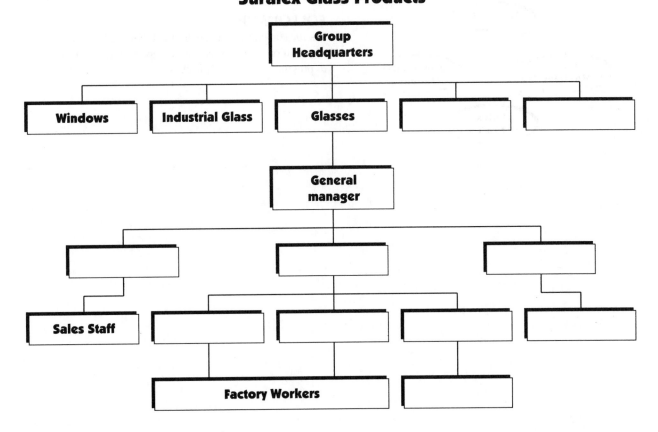

© Macmillan Publishers Limited 1995.

PHOTOCOPIABLE

Company structure **Worksheet Progress check** 1–5a **and** 1–5b

NOTE: Use Worksheets 1–5a and 1–5b for this activity.

ACTIVITY
Pairwork: reading, speaking

AIMS
To talk about company organisation, people's responsibilities and who they report to.

GRAMMAR AND FUNCTIONS
Present simple and present continuous
Adjectival phrases: *responsible for, in charge of + -ing*

VOCABULARY
Responsibility: *to be responsible for, to be in charge of, to deal with, to supervise*
Organisation: *a department, a division, headquarters, a team*
Job titles and functions

PREPARATION
Make a copy of Worksheet 1–5a for each student in the class, and one copy of Worksheet 1–5b for every two students in the class. Cut out Student A and Student B sections as indicated.

TIME
40 minutes

PROCEDURE
1 Draw a small diagram on the board like the one below and elicit/teach the forms:

responsible for... -ing
be in charge of... -ing
deals with something
reports to
has ... under him/her
helps somebody with something
His/Her job is to...
supervise

2 Give each student a copy of Worksheet 1–5a. Cut Worksheet 1–5b in half as indicated. Ask the students to work in pairs and divide them into Student A and Student B. Give each student the appropriate section of the worksheet.

3 Ask each student to work alone, and complete the chart on Worksheet 1–5a using the information in the texts.

4 When they have finished, ask students to put away the text and, using only the completed chart, to explain the organisation of their company to their partner. They should not show the chart to their partner. As they explain it, their partner should fill in the blank chart on his/her worksheet.

5 When they have done this, ask the students to show each other the chart they completed earlier to check they have completed it correctly.

6 Draw the completed charts in the Teacher's Notes on the board or put them on an OHP for the students to check their answers.

FOLLOW-UP
Ask the students to prepare for the following lesson an organisation chart of their own company or an imaginary one to present to the rest of the class.

© Macmillan Publishers Limited 1995.

Descriptions

Student A

Royal Swedish Crystal

Royal Swedish Crystal
(Chief Designer)

RSC is a small company which produces high-quality glasses and sells these all around the world. There are 18 employees and the Managing Director. He is responsible for sales and marketing and has under him a sales team of three: one Export Sales Manager and two sales representatives. The office staff deal with orders and give secretarial help to the Managing Director.

As Chief Designer, you are in charge of the design department and your job is to make new designs and to organise the work of the production department. You are also responsible for quality. There are two other designers under you. There is no Production Manager: the team of nine glass makers report to you and to the Managing Director.

Student B

Suralex Glass Products

(Production Manager)

You work in the Glasses Division of Suralex SA. There are four other divisions in the Suralex Group: Windows, Industrial Glass, Laboratory Equipment and Windscreens. The Glasses Division employs 110 people in the production and sales of the glasses. Central departments at the group's headquarters deal with the marketing and administrative work. As Production Manager you are responsible for organising and

planning production. There are three people under you: two Production Foremen who supervise the factory workers, and the Factory Manager who is responsible for stores and transport staff. The Development Manager and the one designer under him design new products. Like the Sales Manager and the Development Manager you report directly to the General Manager.

© Macmillan Publishers Limited 1995.

PHOTOCOPIABLE

Company structure Worksheet Progress 1-5b

ANSWERS

Royal Swedish Crystal

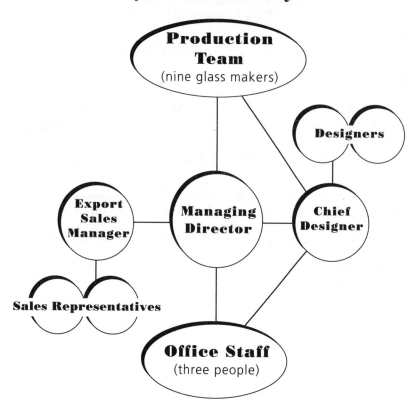

Suralex Glass Products

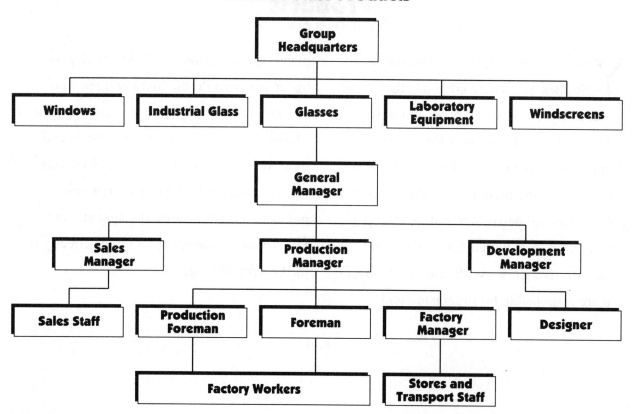

© Macmillan Publishers Limited 1995.

Student A

leave/Navy and move/South America	meet/Claudia Bello, film maker/South America
train as/communications officer	graduate/university/electronics
set up/TV company	travel/world
join/Navy	be born/Paris/1958

✂

Student B

leave/school/16	meet/Vladimir Grinkov, communications expert
work/photographer's studio	set up/TV company
leave/job and go/art school	win/film competition
make/first film	be born/Buenos Aires/1960

© Macmillan Publishers Limited 1995.

Two careers Worksheet

ACTIVITY
Pairwork or groupwork: speaking, writing

AIM
To talk about a person's background and career.

GRAMMAR AND FUNCTIONS
Past simple: regular and irregular verbs

VOCABULARY
Education and work history: *to work, to join, to graduate, to train as, to leave (school/job), to move, to set up, to win, to go to (school, college), to travel*
Linking events: *one day, then, after that, later, so*

PREPARATION
Make one copy of the worksheet for each pair of students in the class. Cut out Student A and Student B sections as indicated.

TIME
40 minutes

PROCEDURE
1 Divide the class into two groups of Student As and Student Bs and ask the students to work with a partner from the same group. Give each pair the appropriate part of the worksheet.

2 Ask students to match the prompts to the pictures.

3 When they have done this, ask them to put them in a logical order. (There is more than one possible order.)

4 Still in their pairs, ask them to practise telling the story to their partner, using the prompts to make full sentences. Go round and help them with prepositions and linking words, but do not change their order of the events.

5 Put the students into new pairs, one Student A with one Student B, and ask them to tell each other their different stories, keeping their worksheets covered.

6 Ask students to say what the link is between the two stories.

7 Check the versions of the two stories with the whole class and ask the students to write one of them.

FOLLOW-UP
Ask the students either to prepare and present their own educational background and work history, or to interview another student and present that person's life history.

SUGGESTED ANSWERS

He was born in Paris in 1958.

He graduated from university in Electronics.

He joined the Navy.

He trained as a communications officer.

He travelled all over the world.

He left the Navy and moved to South America.

In South America he met Claudia Bello, a film maker.

They set up a TV company.

She was born in Buenos Aires in 1960.

She left school at 16.

She worked in a photographer's studio.

She left her job and went to art school.

She made her first film.

She won a film competition.

She met Vladimir Grinkov, a communications expert.

They set up a TV company.

© Macmillan Publishers Limited 1995.

Questions

Question	Question	Question
Did you pay the invoice from the cleaning company?	Did you prepare the programme for the conference?	Did you reserve a room for Mr Simons?
Did you type my speech for next week's conference?	Did you find out the address of the Swiss ambassador?	Did you order more paper for the photocopier?
Did you pick up the envelopes with the new company logo from the printing company?	Did you find the memo from Head Office about salaries?	Did you show Ms Ingram around the building yesterday?
Did you book my flight to Tokyo?	Did you cancel my meeting with Mr Howard next week?	Did you listen to the phone messages when you arrived this morning?
Did you wait for an answer to the fax that we sent to Canada?	Did you telephone Mr da Silva in Brazil?	Did you deliver the report to Jane Buckley?
Did you file the letter from Harry Naylor?	Did you answer the enquiry about spare parts?	Did you explain to the new receptionist how to use the switchboard?
Did you give Helen Harmer the money for her travel expenses?	Did you meet Maria Marquez at the airport?	Did you solve the problem with the computer?
Did you make a copy of the article about us in yesterday's newspaper?	Did you reserve a table at Michel's restaurant for me?	Did you confirm my appointment with the President of NFK?

© Macmillan Publishers Limited 1995.

PHOTOCOPIABLE

Office work Worksheets and

NOTE: Use Worksheets Progress Check 7a and 7b for this activity.

ACTIVITY
Pairwork or groupwork: speaking

AIM
To ask and answer questions about routine administrative work.

GRAMMAR AND FUNCTIONS
Past simple: questions and negatives; short answers:
    Yes, I did/No, I didn't
Regular and irregular verbs
Explaining: *I couldn't ... I had to ...*

VOCABULARY
Routine office and secretarial duties: *to reserve, to book, to cancel, to confirm, an appointment, a meeting, a flight, to pay, to order, an invoice, a receipt, to pick up, to deliver, spare parts; to telephone, to meet, to listen to, to show around, to type, to file, to answer, to make a copy of, a letter, an enquiry, a memo, an article, to wait for, to solve, to find, to find out, to prepare, a programme, a problem, travel expenses, a message*
Explanations: *booked, late, not available, in a hurry, wrong, not in stock, broken*

PREPARATION
Make one copy of Worksheet 7a (questions) and one copy of Worksheet 7b (answers) for each group of two to four students. Cut out the cards as indicated, keeping the two piles of question and answer cards separate. Shuffle each pile.

TIME
30 minutes

PROCEDURE

1 Elicit from the students the duties and daily tasks of a secretary or personal assistant.

2 Tell the students that they are going to play a game in which they will ask a secretary if he/she did a particular job yesterday.

3 Ask students to work in groups of two, three or four.

4 Give each group one set of question cards and one set of answer cards.

5 Before the students start playing the game, explain how to play using the instructions on the back of Worksheet 7b. If you wish, you can photocopy these instructions and distribute a copy to each group, or display a copy on an overhead projector.

6 When the first student reaches the end of the game, ask all the groups to stop playing, even if they have not finished. In each group, the student who has discarded all the answer cards is the winner.

© Macmillan Publishers Limited 1995.

Answers

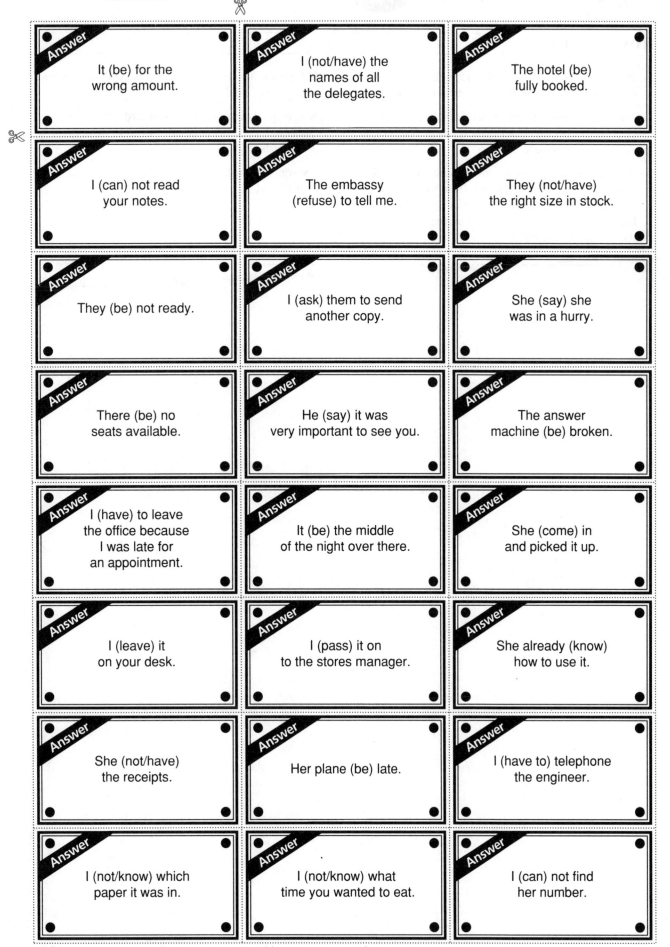

Answer	Answer	Answer
It (be) for the wrong amount.	I (not/have) the names of all the delegates.	The hotel (be) fully booked.
I (can) not read your notes.	The embassy (refuse) to tell me.	They (not/have) the right size in stock.
They (be) not ready.	I (ask) them to send another copy.	She (say) she was in a hurry.
There (be) no seats available.	He (say) it was very important to see you.	The answer machine (be) broken.
I (have) to leave the office because I was late for an appointment.	It (be) the middle of the night over there.	She (come) in and picked it up.
I (leave) it on your desk.	I (pass) it on to the stores manager.	She already (know) how to use it.
She (not/have) the receipts.	Her plane (be) late.	I (have to) telephone the engineer.
I (not/know) which paper it was in.	I (not/know) what time you wanted to eat.	I (can) not find her number.

© Macmillan Publishers Limited 1995.

PHOTOCOPIABLE

Office work   **Worksheet**

HOW TO PLAY

1   Place the question cards face down in a pile in the middle of the table. Give out all the answer cards to the players.

2   Player 1 turns over the first question card and asks the player on his/her left (Player 2) the question. For example: *Did you book my flight to Tokyo?*

3   Player 2 now looks at his/her answer cards for a suitable answer. For example: *No, I didn't. There were no seats available* and throws away that answer card. (Note that he/she will also have to form the negative past tense from the infinitive on the card.)

If Player 2 cannot find an appropriate answer card, he/she must say, Yes, I did.

4   Now Player 2 turns over a question card and asks the question. The teacher must judge when an answer is unacceptable.

5   The winner is the first player to have no answer cards left in their hand.

© Macmillan Publishers Limited 1995.

Student A

Datasoft Inc	Last year	Year before
Turnover		
Countries		
Number of products sold		
Market share (domestic)		
Market share (world)		
New products		
Number of employees		

CasaFina SA	Last year	Year before
Turnover	Pta. 4 billion	Pta. 3 billion
Countries	18	13
Number of products sold	12,500	11,000
Market share (domestic)	16%	16%
Market share (world)	4%	3.7%
New products	7	0
Number of employees	850	800

Allen Greenburg
President

Last year Datasoft Inc's turnover ——————— (be) $ ——————— , a decrease of $ ———————

from the year before. They ——————— (sell) over ——————— products in ——————— different

countries. Their share of the domestic market ——————— (go) down by ——————— % to

——————— % and they ——————— (have) a ——————— % share of the world market. During

the year they ——————— (launch) ——————— new products.

At the same time they ——————— (reduce) their number of employees by ——————— from

——————— to ——————— .

© Macmillan Publishers Limited 1995.

Dealing with figures Worksheets and

NOTE: Use Worksheets 8a and 8b for this activity.

ACTIVITY
Pairwork: speaking, writing

AIM
To report facts and statistics about a company.

GRAMMAR AND FUNCTIONS
Past simple: question forms; regular verbs
Prepositions with statistics: *from, to, by, at, of*

VOCABULARY
Statistics: *to increase, to go up, to go down, to stay the same, to reduce; market share, product, domestic/world (market), employees, staff, turnover, an increase, to export, to launch, to sell (sold)*
Numbers: *hundred, thousand, million, billion, one point two, seventy per cent*

PREPARATION
Make copies of Worksheet 8a and Worksheet 8b and divide them equally among the class.

TIME
30 minutes

PROCEDURE

1 Write a few numbers on the board and check that the students can say them: 1.4 (one point four), 6,500 (six thousand five hundred), 64,000,000 (sixty-four million), 5,206 (five thousand, two hundred and six), 88% (eighty-eight per cent), ½ (a half), ⅓ (a third), ¼ (a quarter).

2 Ask the students to work in pairs and divide the students into Student A and Student B. Give a copy of the worksheet marked Student A to each Student A and a copy of the worksheet marked Student B to each Student B. Ask the students to look at the completed grids on their worksheet. Explain that they work for this company. Tell them that they must complete the blank grid by asking their partner questions in the past tense.
For example:
    What was Datasoft's turnover last year?
    And what was it the year before that?
    How many countries did CasaFina sell their
    products in?
Elicit the questions for the other categories.

3 Ask the students to exchange their information and, by asking and answering questions, to complete their grid.

4 Check the answers with the whole class.

5 In the same pairs they should now complete the passage at the bottom of each worksheet.

6 Again, check the answers with the whole class.

FOLLOW-UP
Ask the students to record similar facts about their own company, or a company they know well, and to write a description like the one on their worksheet.

© Macmillan Publishers Limited 1995.

Student B

Datasoft Inc	Last year	Year before
Turnover	$32 billion	$36 billion
Countries	42	40
Number of products sold	1.9 million	2.4 million
Market share (domestic)	48%	56%
Market share (world)	30%	38%
New products	0	16
Number of employees	4000	6000

CasaFina SA	Last year	Year before
Turnover		
Countries		
Number of products sold		
Market share (domestic)		
Market share (world)		
New products		
Number of employees		

Consuela Rodriguez
Director

Last year CasaFina SA ———————— (increase) their turnover by ——————— % from

Pta ——————— to Pta ———————. They ——————— (sell) ——————— products and

——————— (export) to ——————— different countries. Their share of the domestic market

——————— (stay) the same at ———————, but their share of the world market ——————— (go)

up from ——————— % to ——————— %. They ——————— (launch) ——————— new

products and ——————— (employ) ——————— new staff. The total number of employees

——————— (be) ——————— last year.

© Macmillan Publishers Limited 1995.

PHOTOCOPIABLE

Dealing with figures **Worksheet** *8b*

ANSWERS

Student A

Last year Datasoft Inc's turnover was $32 billion, a decrease of $4 million from the year before. They sold over 1.9 million products in 42 different countries. Their share of the domestic market went down by 8% to 48% and they had a 30% share of the world market. During the year they launched no new products. At the same time they reduced their number of employees by 2,000 from 6,000 to 4,000.

Student B

Last year CasaFina SA increased their turnover by 50% from Pta. 3 billion to Pta. 4 billion. They sold 12,500 products and exported to l8 different countries. Their share of the domestic market stayed the same at l6%, but their share of the world market went up from 3.7% to 4%. They launched 7 new products and employed 50 new staff. The total number of employees was 850 last year.

© Macmillan Publishers Limited 1995.

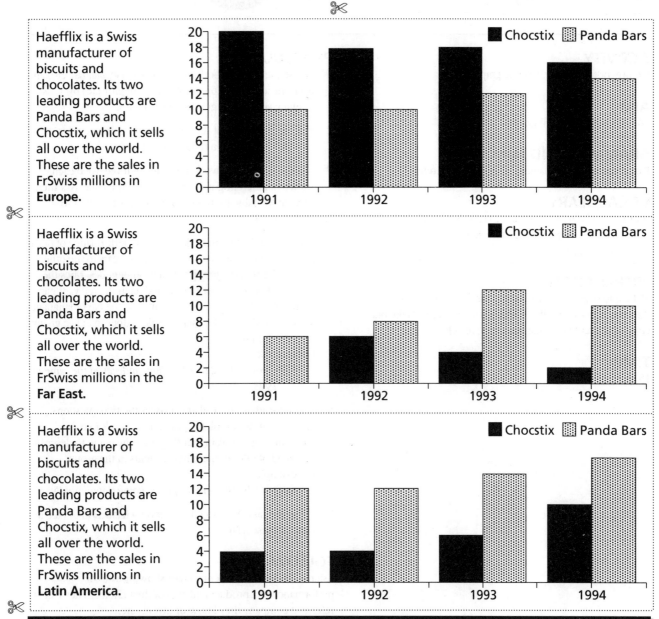

Haefflix is a Swiss manufacturer of biscuits and chocolates. Its two leading products are Panda Bars and Chocstix, which it sells all over the world. These are the sales in FrSwiss millions in **Europe.**

Haefflix is a Swiss manufacturer of biscuits and chocolates. Its two leading products are Panda Bars and Chocstix, which it sells all over the world. These are the sales in FrSwiss millions in the **Far East.**

Haefflix is a Swiss manufacturer of biscuits and chocolates. Its two leading products are Panda Bars and Chocstix, which it sells all over the world. These are the sales in FrSwiss millions in **Latin America.**

Product and Year		Europe	Far East	Latin America	Total
Chocstix	**1991**				
	1992				
	1993				
	1994				
Panda Bars	**1991**				
	1992				
	1993				
	1994				

1 What are the trends in sales of Chocstix: a in Europe?
  b in the Far East?
  c in Latin America?
  d in the world?

2 What are the trends in sales of Panda Bars: a in Europe?
  b in the Far East?
  c in Latin America?
  d in the world?

© Macmillan Publishers Limited 1995.

PHOTOCOPIABLE

Describing performance **Worksheet** 9

ACTIVITY
Groupwork: speaking, reading graphs

AIM
To interpret charts and graphs.

GRAMMAR AND FUNCTIONS
Past simple; present continuous to describe trends

VOCABULARY
Statistics: *to increase, to go up, to go down, to decrease,*
to rise, to fall, to stay the same, to remain stable, rapidly,
steadily, slightly

PREPARATION
Make one copy of the worksheet for every three students in
the class. Cut out the three sections as indicated. Make one
copy of the table for each student in the class.

TIME
15 minutes

PROCEDURE
1 Revise the verbs of performance (*increase, fall, rise* etc) and
elicit the adverbs of degree (*rapidly, slightly* etc) by
drawing simple line graphs on the board.

2 Tell the students that they are going to compare sales of
two chocolate bars in three different areas.

3 Ask the students to work in groups of three. Give each
student a different graph and a copy of the table. Ask them
to fill in the table for their area without showing it to
their partners.

4 Now ask each student to describe the performance of both
products in their area over the last four years to the other
two students in the group. As each student describes the
performance, the other two should fill in the relevant part
of the table. Make sure the students use the target language
to describe the development of sales rather than just giving
a series of numbers.
For example:
> *Sales rose in 1992 to 12 million, and stayed the same in*
> *1993.*

5 Ask the students to read and answer the two questions,
under the now-completed grid, about trends in the
different areas. Explain that they are now going to describe
the trend of sales to the other students in the group.
For example:
> *Sales of Chocstix in Europe are going down rapidly.*

6 If you like, ask them to comment on what action to take in
view of these trends.

FOLLOW-UP
Ask the students to present a chart showing sales or
performance of a product and area of their choice. They can
refer to a company they know or invent one.

ANSWERS

Product and Year		Europe	Far East	Latin America	Total
Chocstix	1991	20	0	4	24
	1992	18	6	4	28
	1993	18	4	6	28
	1994	16	2	10	28
Panda Bars	1991	10	6	12	28
	1992	10	8	12	30
	1993	12	12	14	38
	1994	14	10	16	40

© Macmillan Publishers Limited 1995.

Student A

CYRUS COMPUTER SYSTEMS

Turnover	$180 million	**Products**	Range of approx. 10 PCs at any one time
			Software solutions: mainly financial programme
Employees	560	**Divisions**	Hardware, Software and systems, Repair and maintenance

Offices	Headquarters and research centre in Birmingham, UK
	Software consultants in London, Birmingham and Manchester
Factories	One manufacturing plant in Scotland
	Repair workshop and warehouse in Birmingham
Sales Offices	Dealers in all major UK cities
Subsidiaries	None
Agents	France, Spain, Portugal and Italy; service agreements with local companies

COMPANY PROFILE

Which company and where?
Main activities?
What products or services?
Factories?
Which countries / markets?
Size of company?
Other companies in group?

✂ ....

Student B

NIHON MEDICINE COMPANY

Turnover	1.2 billion	**Employees**	218

Activity	Sales of pharmaceutical products, market research and testing of products
Divisions	General medicine – leading brand: Sanadol (aspirin)
	Prescription drugs – leading brand: Biozedon (tranquilliser)
Office	Headquarters in Nagoya
	Parent company in Düsseldorf, Germany with factories in Essen and Düsseldorf
	Other subsidiary in US (sales only, not manufacturing)
Markets	Japan and Far East
Sales Offices	Nagoya, Tokyo and Singapore

COMPANY PROFILE

Which company and where?
Main activities?
What products or services?
Factories?
Which countries / markets?
Size of company?
Other companies in group?

© Macmillan Publishers Limited 1995.

PHOTOCOPIABLE

Company profile Worksheet *10*

ACTIVITY
Pairwork: speaking

AIM
To talk about the various parts of a large company; its
divisions, subsidiaries, etc.

GRAMMAR AND FUNCTIONS
Have got, there is/are
Basic question forms

VOCABULARY
Parts of a company: *a division, a sales office, a factory,
an agent, a subsidiary, a dealer, headquarters,
a parent company*

PREPARATION
Make one copy of the worksheet for each pair of students in
the class. Cut out Student A and Student B sections as
indicated.

TIME
30 minutes

PROCEDURE

1 Discuss the various operations/divisions of a large
multinational like Coca-Cola to elicit some of the vocabulary.

2 Tell the students they are going to look at the operations of
two other companies.

3 Ask the students to work in pairs and divide them into
Student A and Student B. Give each student the appropriate
part of the worksheet.

4 Focus the students' attention on the table at the bottom of
their worksheet and elicit the type of question they will
need to ask to find the necessary information.
For example:
> *What is the company? Where is it based?*

5 Ask the students to study the information about the
company at the top of their worksheet.

6 When they are ready, ask the students to question each
other about the two companies and fill in the table as
they do so.

7 When all the pairs have completed their charts, discuss the
differences and similarities between the two companies
with the whole class.
For example:
> *Cyrus is a manufacturing company, but Nihon Medicine
> is a sales company. Cyrus hasn't got any
> subsidiaries; Nihon Medicine has a subsidiary.*

FOLLOW-UP
Ask the students to prepare a description of a company they
know well and get the other students to ask questions about it
as before, but without using their grids.

ANSWERS

Student A
Company Profile

Which company and where?	Nihon Medicine Company – Headquarters Nagoya. Parent company, Düsseldorf, Germany
Main activities?	Sale of pharmaceutical products, market research and testing
What products or services?	Selling general medicines and prescription drugs
Factories?	Essen and Dusseldorf
Which countries/markets?	Japan and Far East
Size of company?	218 employees
Other companies in group?	Subsidiary in US (sales only, not manufacturing)

Student B
Company Profile

Which company and where?	Cyrus Computer Systems, Birmingham, UK
Main activities?	Manufacturing of PCs, hardware and software programmes
What products or services?	Range of 10 PCs at any one time – Software solutions, mainly financial programmes
Factories?	Scotland
Which countries/markets?	Agents in France, Spain, Portugal and Italy
Size of company?	560 employees
Other companies in group?	None

© Macmillan Publishers Limited 1995.

Student A

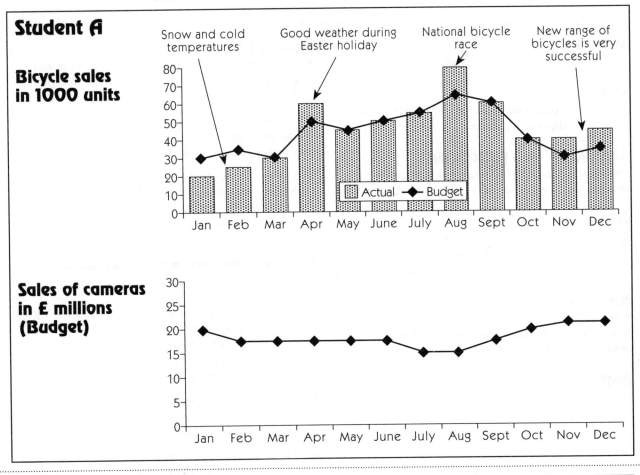

Bicycle sales in 1000 units

Snow and cold temperatures

Good weather during Easter holiday

National bicycle race

New range of bicycles is very successful

Actual — Budget

Sales of cameras in £ millions (Budget)

Student B

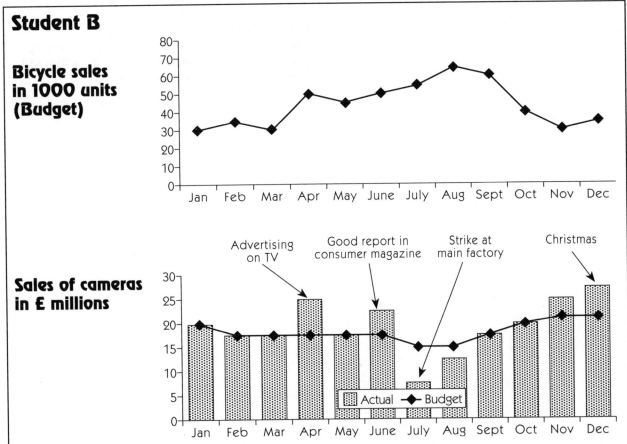

Bicycle sales in 1000 units (Budget)

Sales of cameras in £ millions

Advertising on TV

Good report in consumer magazine

Strike at main factory

Christmas

Actual — Budget

© Macmillan Publishers Limited 1995.

PHOTOCOPIABLE

Meeting the budget Worksheet Progress check   6-10

ACTIVITY
Pairwork: speaking, interpreting graphs

AIM
To talk about performance using a graph, and to explain the reasons for changes in performance.

GRAMMAR AND FUNCTIONS
Revision of past tense forms (questions and negative)
Giving reasons: *because of, due to, as a result, because of this*

VOCABULARY
Budgeting: *budget, to plan, actual, sales, to reach a target, units, a range, actually, successful*
General: *a strike, a newspaper report, spare parts*

PREPARATION
Make one copy of the worksheet for each pair of students in the class. Cut out Student A and Student B sections as indicated.

TIME
45 minutes

PROCEDURE

1   Ask the students to work in pairs and divide them into Student A and Student B. Give each student the appropriate part of the worksheet.

2   Focus the students' attention on the graphs and explain that they have the budget figures for their partner's company, but not the actual sales figures.

3   Explain that they must find out from their partner whether his/her company actually sold what it planned to in the budget. The students should look at the various statements above the actual figures to see the reasons for the rise or fall in anticipated sales.

4   Ask the students to look at 'Bicycle sales' and use a Student A to model the activity.
For example:
> You: *You planned to sell 30,000 units in January. What did you actually sell?*
> Student A: *We only sold 20,000 units.*
> You: *Why was that?*
> Student A: *Because of the cold weather.*

5   Ask the students to ask and answer similar questions. They should draw in the columns showing the actual figures as they get the information from their partner.

6   When the students have finished, ask them to look at their partner's graph to check their answers.

FOLLOW-UP
Ask the students to present a graph to the class, describing the changes that took place and the reasons for them. (Financial newspapers can be a good source for these.)

rmillan Publishers Limited 1995.

Student A
JOB 1 Advertising Sales, Management Now magazine

You work in the advertising department of *Management Now*, a weekly magazine. It has three sections: financial and economic, management, and industrial news. Your job is to take calls from people who want to place advertisements in the magazine and write down the details.

JOB 2 General Manager, Transworld Express

You work for Transworld Express, a courier company which delivers business letters and parcels all over the world. You would like to advertise your services in an international business newspaper. Your budget is $6,000. Telephone *International Business News* newspaper, and place an advertisement.

ADVERTISEMENT BOOKING FORM

Date of advertisement			
Page/section of magazine	Financial & economic	Management	Industrial news
Size of advertisement	☐ Full page ($800/week)	☐ Half page ($400/week)	☐ Quarter page ($200/week)
Number of weeks			
Text of advertisement			
Graphics	☐ Yes ☐ No	Details	
Colour/black & white	☐ Black & white	☐ Colour	
Payment	☐ Cheque	☐ Credit card	☐ Account

✂

Student B
JOB 1 Advertising Sales, International Business News

You work in the advertising department of *International Business News*, a daily newspaper.

Your job is to take calls from people who want to place advertisements in the magazine and to write down the details. Next week there is a special transport section in the newspaper.

ADVERTISEMENT BOOKING FORM

Date of advertisement			
Page/section of newspaper	Main section	Transport section	
Size of advertisement	☐ Full page ($600 a day)	☐ Half page ($400 a day)	☐ Quarter page ($200 a day)
Number of days			
Text of advertisement			
Graphics	☐ Yes ☐ No	Details	
Colour/black & white	☐ Black & white	☐ Colour	
Payment	☐ Cheque	☐ Credit card	☐ Account

JOB 2 Office Manager, *Friedrich and Hassler Accountants*

You work for a firm of accountants which gives financial advice to companies. You would like to advertise your services in *Management Now* magazine. Your budget is $8,000. Telephone them and place an advertisement.

© Macmillan Publishers Limited 1995.

PHOTOCOPIABLE

Placing an advertisement Worksheet 11

ACTIVITY
Pairwork: speaking, writing

AIM
To make specific requests and to fill in a form.

GRAMMAR AND FUNCTIONS
Verbs taking the infinitive: *would like to, need to, want to*
Questions: *When? What? Which? How? How many? How big?*

VOCABULARY
Newspaper advertising: *text, full/half/quarter page, section, graphics, details*
Payment: *by cheque, by credit card, on account*

PREPARATION
Make one copy of the worksheet for each pair of students in the class. Cut out Student A and Student B sections as indicated.
You might like to collect some classified advertisements from newspapers and magazines and bring them in to class.

TIME
25 minutes

PROCEDURE
1 If you like, take in some newspaper or magazine classified advertisements to show the students. Ask them what kind of things you have to think about before placing an advertisement. For example: *the size of the ad, the text, the artwork* etc.

2 Ask the students to work in pairs and divide them into Student A and Student B. Give each student the appropriate part of the worksheet.

3 Ask the students to read the information for Job 1 on the worksheet and then look at the Advertising Booking Form. Elicit the correct questions for each box on the form. For example:
  When would you like to put the advertisement in the paper?
  Which section of the paper would you like it to go in?
  What would you like it to say?
  Do you want to have graphics? etc.

4 Ask the students to look at Job 2 on the worksheet. Explain that they are going to take it in turns to place an advertisement. Ask them to think for a few minutes about the kind of advertisement they would like to place and what they would like it to say.

5 When they are ready, ask the students to play the roles of advertiser and customer, making sure that the advertiser fills in the form.

6 When they have finished, ask each student to report back briefly to the class on the kind of advertisement their partner wanted to place.

FOLLOW-UP
Ask the students to interview each other about their own companies, a school or a fictional company and, using this information, make a short advertisement for their 'client'.

© Macmillan Publishers Limited 1995.

Reward Pre-intermediate
Business Resource Pack

	You	Your partner
Employment		
1 Employees will work shorter hours.		
2 The number of manual jobs will decrease.		
3 A lot of people will work from home.		
4 People will retire later.		
5 Employees will be multi-skilled (ie do several different jobs).		
6 People will stay with the same employer for life.		
7 There will not be so many levels of management.		
Trade		
8 China will lead the world in manufacturing.		
9 There will be free trade between all countries.		
10 Developing countries will overtake the 'industrial West'.		
11 Industrial pollution will not be a great problem.		
12 Many small companies will disappear; the big ones will survive.		
13 There will be a single world currency.		
14 National governments will not have control of major industries like energy and defence.		

© Macmillan Publishers Limited 1995.

The business world 2010   Worksheet   12

ACTIVITY
Pairwork and groupwork: speaking

AIM
To talk about future trends in employment and trade.

GRAMMAR AND FUNCTIONS
Will for prediction
Agreement and disagreement

VOCABULARY
Employment: *to retire, to stay with, to work from home, a manual job, multi-skilled, long/short hours, an employer, an employee*
Economics: *to disappear, to survive, to lead, to overtake, to have control of, free trade, a currency, energy, defence, a developing country, single*

PREPARATION
Make one copy of the worksheet for each student in the class.

TIME
30 minutes

PROCEDURE

1 Ask students to imagine how work will be different in the future.

2 Write up the following statement:
    In the future robots will replace people at work.

3 Ask the students to comment on this idea and elicit the language of agreement and disagreement.

4 Give a worksheet to each student and ask them to read the 'Employment' section, statements 1–7. Explain to the students that they must decide whether or not they agree with the statements and fill in the column marked 'you' accordingly.

5 When they have finished, put the students into pairs and ask them to discuss these same statements with their partner. As they do so, they should fill in the column marked 'your partner'.

6 When they have done this, open a class discussion on the students' opinions.

7 Repeat this procedure with the 'Trade' section, statements 8–14. Students could be put into different pairs, if you wish.

8 Open a class discussion on the students' opinions. Were they in agreement with their partner or not?

FOLLOW-UP
Ask the students to write a short article for a business magazine on the business world in 2010. They could choose to focus on their own particular field of work or industry.

© Macmillan Publishers Limited 1995.

Reward Pre-intermediate
Business Resource Pack

perfume

shampoo

1 There are so many competitors in this market; it's difficult to know the right strategy. We want to reach as many people as possible. So we're going to advertise it as a family product. This means we're going to sell it in large bottles and keep the price low. But first people need to know about it. We're going to send free samples to half a million homes so that they can try it out for themselves.

2 This product is different from other brands on the market. It tastes nice, which is important for children, but it doesn't have sugar in it. We need to have the help of doctors and pharmacists to sell this idea to the customer. So we're going to present the product to groups of doctors when we launch it at the Healthcare Exhibition in Geneva. We are also going to produce it in a number of unusual colours like purple, black and green. Children will love this and will remember the product.

artificial sweetener

3 Who are the customers for this kind of product? They are professional people who like good food and wine. But at the same time they want to be fit and healthy. We're going to sponsor a number of top sporting events and advertise in professional magazines. We want to create an image of a healthy, up-market product, which people can buy instead of wine.

lipstick

cough medicine

health drink

washing powder

© Macmillan Publishers Limited 1995.

PHOTOCOPIABLE

A marketing campaign Worksheet 13a

NOTE: This activity is not linked to the activity on Worksheet 13b.

ACTIVITY
Pairwork and groupwork: reading and speaking

AIM
To plan and present a marketing campaign for a product.

GRAMMAR AND FUNCTIONS
Stating intentions: *going to, want to, need to*

VOCABULARY
Marketing: *to reach, to launch, to sponsor, to create an image, a product, a free sample, a strategy, a competitor, a brand, healthy, up-market, low (price), professional, purple*

PREPARATION
Make one copy of the worksheet for each student in the class.

TIME
30 minutes

PROCEDURE

1 Pre-teach the vocabulary. Give each student a worksheet and make sure they understand what the different products are.

2 Ask the students to work in pairs and to match each marketing plan with one of the products.

3 When they have done this, compare and discuss their answers with the whole class.

Answers
1 shampoo
2 cough medicine
3 health drink

4 Now ask the students to work in groups of three or four. They must create a marketing plan for one of the other three products. Tell them to use the pre-taught vocabulary and the marketing plans on the worksheets to help them.

5 When the students have finished their marketing plans, ask each group to present their plan to the rest of the class. If you like, you can ask them not to reveal which product is being described and ask the other groups to guess.

FOLLOW-UP
Ask the students to write a marketing plan for a product they know well or for the one they have just presented.

© Macmillan Publishers Limited 1995.

Student A

Make the call

1 Telephone Damask Fabrics Ltd
   Ask for Michelle Rose
   You want to meet her next week to look at her new designs.

2 Telephone Banco Nacional
   Ask for the manager
   You want to speak to him in person.

3 Telephone Spartak Industries
   Ask for Jan Novak
   You want to know his decision before tomorrow. It is now 6 pm and you are going home.

4 Telephone Hoffman Electronics
   Ask for the Sales Department
   You want a copy of their new catalogue and price list.

5 Telephone Jacob Braun AG
   Ask for Judith Schultz
   You want to change your order for labels from 1,000 to 1,200.

6 Telephone the Wing Lok Chinese Restaurant
   You want to book a table for six people for 8.30 pm tonight.

Receive the call

1 SAS Airlines. First check the timetable. There are two flights to Stockholm tomorrow evening: one at 6.45 and one at 9.20. Ask the caller which one he/she would like.

2 Hayashi Steel Company. Put the caller through to Mr Namura's secretary. Now you are Mr Namura's secretary. Check his diary and then tell the caller that Mr Namura is free on Wednesday evening.

3 QTM Photocopiers. Put the caller through to the Service Department. Now you are a service engineer. Apologise and offer to send someone immediately.

4 Travelflora. You are a sales assistant. Ask the caller what kind of flowers he/she would like. You have lilies, roses and tulips.

5 Panyotis Yoghurt. Put the caller through to Athena Vlakhou. Now you are Athena Vlakhou. Listen to what the caller asks for and offer to visit him/her with the samples.

6 Beltrak Railroad Company. You are the receptionist. John Gruber is on holiday this week. Ask if you can take a message.

Student B

Make the call

1 Telephone SAS Airlines
   You want to book a flight to Stockholm tomorrow evening after 5 pm.

2 Telephone Hayashi Steel Company
   Ask for Mr Namura's secretary
   You want to invite him to dinner one evening next week. When you know which day, offer to pick him up at six from his office.

3 Telephone QTM Photocopiers
   Ask for the Service Department
   You want to know why your photocopier breaks down every two days.

4 Telephone Travelflora
   You want to send some flowers to a colleague who had a baby this morning.

5 Telephone Panyotis Yoghurt
   Ask for Athena Vlakhou, Marketing Manager
   You want to have some samples of their yoghurt and to know their prices.

6 Telephone Beltrak Railroad Company
   Ask for John G Gruber
   You want to speak to him in person.

Receive the call

1 Damask Fabrics Ltd. Michelle Rose is out of the office today. Take a message.

2 Banco Nacional. Put the caller through to the manager's secretary. Now you are the manager's secretary. The manager is in a meeting. Offer to take a message.

3 Spartak Industries. Jan Novak is working at home today. First offer to help the caller yourself. Then offer to call Mr Novak and get him to telephone the caller. Take the caller's name and number, and ask if it is urgent.

4 Hoffman Electronics. Put the caller through to the Sales Department. Now you are one of the sales staff. Listen to what the caller asks for and offer to post it today.

5 Jacob Braun AG. Judith Schultz is standing next to you. Now you are Judith Schultz. Listen to what the caller asks for and offer to send another 200 labels as soon as possible. Ask for written confirmation of the new order.

6 Wing Lok Chinese Restaurant. You are fully booked at 8.30 pm. Offer the caller a table at 7 pm or 9.30 pm. Write the caller's name.

© Macmillan Publishers Limited 1995.

Getting through Worksheet 13b

NOTE: This activity is not linked to the activity on Worksheet 13a.

ACTIVITY
Pairwork: speaking

AIM
To make short telephone calls and leave messages.

GRAMMAR AND FUNCTIONS
Suggestions: *Would you like to... ? How about... ?*
    Could you... ?
Refusing and accepting

VOCABULARY
Telephoning: *to put someone through, to call, to phone, to call back, to take/leave a message, to speak to, a caller, in person*
General: *to break down, to invite*

PREPARATION
Make one copy of the worksheet for each pair of students in the class. Cut out Student A and Student B sections as indicated.

TIME
40 minutes

PROCEDURE

1 Explain to the students that they are going to take it in turns to make and receive telephone calls.

2 Write up the following prompts on the board:
    Telephone: Oxford Software
    Ask for: The manager
    You want: To confirm your meeting with him next Friday.
Then, with a confident student act out the following dialogue.
    You: *Hello, Oxford Software*
    Student: *Hello, can I speak to the manager, please?*
    You: *One moment. I'll put you through. I'm sorry, he's not in his office. Can I take a message?*
    Student: *Yes, could you tell him that I'll see him next Friday.*

3 Elicit other useful phrases. For example:
    I'll call back later.
    I need to speak to her in person.
    I'll give him the message.
    I'll post it to you today.
    I'll send them as soon as possible.
    We'll come at 9.30.
    Can I help you?

4 Ask the students to work in pairs and divide them into Student A and Student B. Give each student the appropriate part of the worksheet.

5 Tell the students that they are each going to make and receive phone calls according to the instructions on the worksheet.

6 Give the students a few minutes to study the instructions.

7 When they are ready, ask each Student A to sit back-to-back with a Student B, so they cannot see each other, or see each other's worksheet.

8 The students now take it in turns to make and receive calls. As they do this, the students should make a note of the information they are given.

9 When they have finished, ask each pair of students to compare their information to check they have understood each other correctly.

© Macmillan Publishers Limited 1995.

Student A

1 You are at reception. You want to know where you can get a security pass.

2 You are at the security desk. You want to know where meeting room A is.

3 You are in meeting room A. You want to know where the stores are.

4 You are in the stores. You want to know where the telephones are.

5 You are next to the telephones. You want to know where room 201 is.

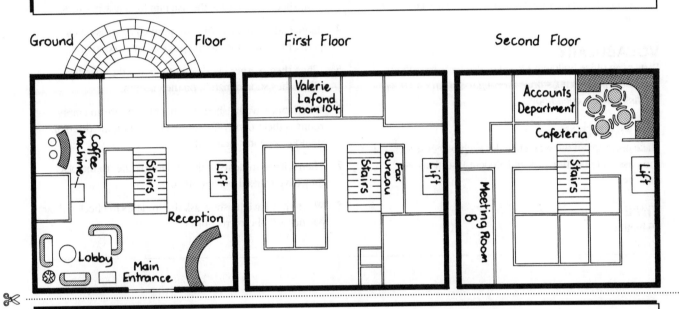

Student B

1 You are at reception. You want to know where Valerie Lafond's office is.

2 You are in Valerie Lafond's office. You want to know where meeting room B is.

3 You are in meeting room B. You want to know where the coffee machine is.

4 You are next to the coffee machine. You want to know where the fax bureau is.

5 You are outside the fax bureau. You want to know where the accounts department is.

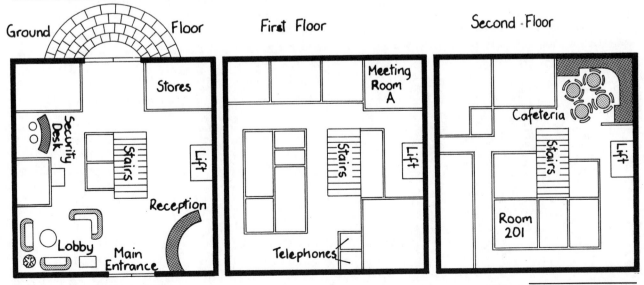

© Macmillan Publishers Limited 1995.

Finding your way **Worksheet** *14*

ACTIVITY
Pairwork: speaking

AIM
To ask for and give directions in and around an office building.

GRAMMAR AND FUNCTIONS
Asking for and giving directions: *Could you tell me where… is?
Could you tell me how to get to… ? Go past, go up, turn
left*

VOCABULARY
Parts of an office building: *lift, stairs, cafeteria, reception,
lobby, fax bureau, stores, meeting room, ground floor,
first floor, second floor*

PREPARATION
Make one copy of the worksheet for each pair of students in
the class. Cut out Student A and Student B sections as
indicated.

TIME
25 minutes

PROCEDURE
1 To model the activity, ask students how to get to various
parts of the building that you are in.

2 Ask the students to work in pairs and divide them into
Student A and Student B. Give each student the appropriate
part of the worksheet.

3 Tell the students to read the instructions at the top of their
worksheet and to study the diagram for a few minutes.

4 Explain that, in their pairs, they are going to ask their
partner for directions to the places they need to find.

5 When their partner has directed them to the specified
place, they should mark it on the diagram.

6 When they have finished, ask them to choose an empty
room as their 'own' office and to mark it on the diagram,
without showing their partner.

7 Then tell the students to direct their partner to the place
they have marked as their office.

8 When they have finished, ask the students to check if their
partner is in the correct place.

© Macmillan Publishers Limited 1995.

A

You work for a book publisher in Canada. You are going on a business trip to Japan. While you are there you will visit a number of agents, teachers at universities, bookshop owners, and someone from the Ministry of Education. Choose some suitable gifts from the list below to take with you.

Excel Promotional Items

	Catalogue No.	Price £
Clothing		
Ties (black, red, green)	1001	6.00
T-shirts (small, medium, large, extra large)	1002	14.00
Umbrellas (golf or ladies')	1003/4	18.00/12.00
Sunglasses	1005	28.00
Silk scarves	1006	17.50
Stationery		
Pens (fountain or ballpoint)	1101/2	8.00/1.00
Desk diary	1103	10.00
Calendars	1105	13.50
Note book	1106	1.75

	Catalogue No.	Price £
Leather goods		
Bookmark (black, red or green)	1201	2.50
Card holder	1203	7.50
Pocket diary	1204	11.00
Games		
Travel chess	1402	4.50
Cards (set of two packs)	1403	3.75
Backgammon	1404	6.00
Accessories		
Watches (for women and men)	1301/2	24.00/26.00
Alarm clock	1303	14.00
Lighters (six different colours)	1304	1.50
Penknives (Swiss Army style)	1305	13.0

B

You work for a company which sells corporate gifts.
You put the customer's name or company logo onto the products you sell.

Excel Promotional Items

Excel Promotional Items	Catalogue No.	Price £	Quantity	Discount	Total £
CLOTHING					
Ties (black, red or green)	1001	6.00			
T-shirts (small, medium, large, extra large)	1002	14.00			
Umbrellas (golf or ladies')	1003/4	18.00/12.00			
Sunglasses	1005	28.00			
Silk scarves	1006	17.50			
STATIONERY					
Pens (fountain or ballpoint)	1101/2	8.00/1.00			
Desk diary	1103	10.00			
Calendars	1105	13.50			
Note book	1106	1.75			
LEATHER GOODS					
Bookmark (black, red or green)	1201	2.50			
Card holder	1203	7.50			
Pocket diary	1204	11.00			
GAMES					
Travel chess	1402	4.50			
Cards (set of two packs)	1403	3.75			
Backgammon	1404	6.00			
ACCESSORIES					
Watches (for women and men)	1301/2	24.00/26.00			
Alarm clock	1303	14.00			
Lighters (six different colours)	1304	1.50			
Penknives (Swiss Army style)	1305	13.00			
TOTAL					

© Macmillan Publishers Limited 1995.

PHOTOCOPIABLE

Placing an order Worksheet 15

ACTIVITY
Pairwork: speaking, filling in an order form

AIM
To place and to receive an order.

GRAMMAR AND FUNCTIONS
Countable and uncountable: *some* and *any*
   How many?
Plural form of nouns
Would like, have got
Dealing with figures

VOCABULARY
Promotional items: *a calendar, a diary, a note book,*
   an umbrella, a silk scarf, sunglasses, clothing, stationery,
   a penknife, a watch

PREPARATION
Make one copy of the worksheet for each pair of students in
the class. Cut out Student A and Student B sections as
indicated.

TIME
30 minutes

PROCEDURE
1   Ask the students to give examples of promotional products
    that can be used to advertise a company. Pre-teach the
    vocabulary.

2   Ask the students to work in pairs and divide them into
    Student A and Student B. Give each student the appropriate
    part of the worksheet.

3   Explain that Student A is a customer and needs to buy some
    promotional gifts while Student B works for a company
    which sells corporate gifts.

4   Ask the Student As to read the descriptions of the people
    they will need gifts for and decide what to get. Ask the
    Student Bs to decide what their discounting policy is going
    to be, that is, how much discount they will allow for
    quantity purchasing and also to imagine that some items
    are out of stock.

5   Model the activity with a more confident student.
    For example:
       You: *I'd like to order some stationery with the
          company's name on it.*
       Student: *What kind of stationery do you want?*
       You: *Have you got any pens?*
       Student: *Yes, we have. How many would you like?*
       You: *Well, how much are they?*
       Student: *They're £8 each.*
       You: *OK, I'll have ten, please.*

6   Ask the students to work in pairs, a Student A with a
    Student B and to sit back-to-back so they cannot see each
    other, or see each other's worksheet.

7   Student A now telephones Student B to place an order.
    Student B should take down the order, filling in the form.

8   When they have finished, ask the students to report back
    on what they have ordered for each client.

FOLLOW-UP
Ask the students to write a fax confirming their order.

© Macmillan Publishers Limited 1995.

11–15 | *The marketing consultant*

Reward Pre-intermediate
Business Resource Pack

You work for 'Imagine', a team of marketing consultants which helps companies to plan marketing campaigns for new products. They find out all the information about the product and then suggest when, where and how to launch it.

	Product 1	Product 2
Type of product		
Name of product		
Start of campaign		
Target customer		
USP		
Price range		
Type of outlet		
Advertising budget		

Student A
Product 1

Micron 2000 is a low-price microscope for young children (11–15) to use at home or at school. It is easy to use and unbreakable. You would like to start selling the product in good time for the beginning of the school year. You sell other microscopes in specialist shops, but because Micron 2000 is made for children, you want to sell it to toy shops and schools. Your budget is £1.5 million.

Student B
Product 2

Boxer Shoes are a new type of shoe for young women (18–30). They are available in only one colour – red – and will look good as sports shoes or as fashion shoes. The price is high, but these shoes have a fashionable image. You would not like to sell them in the usual sports shops, but in more expensive and up-market stores. Your budget is $ 4.8 million.

© Macmillan Publishers Limited 1995.

The marketing consultant Worksheet Progress check *11–15*

ACTIVITY
Pairwork: reading, speaking, making a short presentation

AIM
To gather information and then present a profile of a product and a marketing strategy for it.

GRAMMAR AND FUNCTIONS
Revision of *would like to, want to, going to*
Stating plans and intentions

VOCABULARY
Marketing: *a (marketing) campaign, an outlet, a budget, a target (customer), a USP (unique selling point), a range, a brand name, a catalogue, a supplier, to run a campaign*

PREPARATION
Make one copy of the table for each student in the class. Cut out the Student A and Student B sections as indicated.

TIME
40 minutes

PROCEDURE
1 Give a copy of the table to each student and ask them to read the profile of the Marketing Consultancy company. Explain that they are going to act both as a consultant and as a customer of the consultant.

2 Focus students' attention on the table and go through the items, eliciting the right questions to ask.
  For example:
  What kind of product is it?
  What is the product called?
  When would you like to start the campaign?
  What is different about your product?
  Explain any terms they do not understand.

3 Ask the students to work in pairs and divide them into Student A and Student B. Give each student the appropriate part of the worksheet.

4 Ask the students to read the information on the worksheet about the products and fill in the relevant part of the table.

5 When they have done this, tell the students that they are now going to take it in turns to act as marketing consultant.

6 Ask the Student Bs to act as marketing consultants first. They should ask Student A questions about their product, filling in the table at the same time.

7 Repeat this procedure, but this time with the Student As acting as marketing consultant.

8 When they have finished, ask the students to form new pairs of two Student As and two Student Bs. Ask the Student As to prepare a product profile and marketing strategy for Boxer Shoes, and Student Bs to do the same for Micron 2000.

9 Ask pairs to come together into groups of four, two Student As and two Student Bs, to present their strategy to each other. Alternatively a spokesperson from each pair can present the strategy to the class.

FOLLOW-UP
Ask the students to write up their plan in the form of a marketing consultant's report. For example:
  'Shiana' is a perfume with a strong brand name. It is in the high price range and the target customers are wealthy women in their thirties and forties. We are going to launch a campaign in November, because we want to increase sales at Christmas. We would like to expand the market, so we are going to advertise on television.

ANSWERS

	Product 1	**Product 2**
Type of product	microscope	shoes
Name of product	Micron 2000	Boxer shoes
Start of campaign	beginning of school year	don't know
Target customer	children	young women aged 18 – 30
USP	easy to use/unbreakable	sports and fashion shoe
Price range	low	high
Type of outlet	toy shops/schools	up-market shops
Advertising budget	£1.5 million	$4.8 million

© Macmillan Publishers Limited 1995.

Dates and times

	You	Your partner
1 When does the financial year end in your country?		
2 When is the next public holiday in your country?		
3 What time do offices usually open?		
4 What time do offices usually close?		
5 What time do shops close?		
6 What is the busiest time of year for shops?		
7 When do people eat their main meal?		
8 When do people usually get paid?		
9 When do people usually take their holidays?		
10 When do employees negotiate their pay?		
11 When do large companies recruit new staff?		
12 When do people retire? (men and women)		
13 When did you join your company?		
14 When do you arrive at work?		
15 When is your next meeting?		

I was surprised to hear that in (country/company name) _____
they... _____

© Macmillan Publishers Limited 1995.

PHOTOCOPIABLE

Dates and times Worksheet 16a

NOTE: This activity is not linked to the activity on Worksheet 16b.

ACTIVITY
Pairwork and whole class: speaking

AIM
To talk about times and dates.

GRAMMAR AND FUNCTIONS
Prepositions of time: *in, on, at, around/about*
Present simple questions

VOCABULARY
To negotiate, to recruit
General: *busy, main, a public holiday, to get paid, to take a holiday*

PREPARATION
Make one copy of the worksheet for each student in the class.

TIME
25 minutes

PROCEDURE
1 Ask the students to write down a date and a time of day that is important to them.

2 Ask the students to show their dates and times to another student and to ask him/her to guess what is significant about them.
For example:
> *Is it when you were born? Is it when you leave work every day?* etc

3 Ask students to report back to the rest of the class on what they have found out.

4 Give one worksheet to each student and ask them to study it for a moment. Help students with any unfamiliar vocabulary.

5 Ask the students to read the questions and write down their answers in the column marked 'you'.

6 When they have finished, ask the students to work in pairs and interview each other, writing down their partner's answers.

7 When all the students have finished, discuss their findings with the whole class, asking students to comment on anything they found unusual or surprising.

8 Ask the students to look at questions 3, 4, 5, 9 and 12, and to discuss how they think things will be in the future.

9 Ask the students to complete the sentence at the bottom of the worksheet.

FOLLOW-UP
Ask the students to tell the class about the things which they do during the working week and when they do them. Encourage students to ask questions. If they are not currently in work, give them a job title and get them to imagine the routine.

© Macmillan Publishers Limited 1995.

Student A

Call 1 Receive the call.

It is Monday 6 March. You are Susana Pena, Sales Manager for Gourmet Foods.

March

Monday 6
10-12 Sales meeting

Tuesday 7
leave for Belgium 10 am

Wednesday 8

Thursday 9
return from Belgium 4 pm

Friday 10

Call 2 Make the call.

It is Monday 16 June. You are John O'Brien. Phone Kate Palmer and cancel your appointment tomorrow at 4pm. Make a new appointment.

JUNE

Monday 26 *holiday*

Tuesday 27

Wednesday 28

Thursday 29 *Lunch with Sabori Yamaguchi*

Friday 30

✂ ┄┄┄┄┄┄┄┄┄┄┄┄┄┄┄┄┄┄┄┄┄┄┄┄┄┄

Student B

Call 1 Make the call.

It is Monday 6 March. You are John Wheeler. Phone Susana Pena and make an appointment to see her this week.

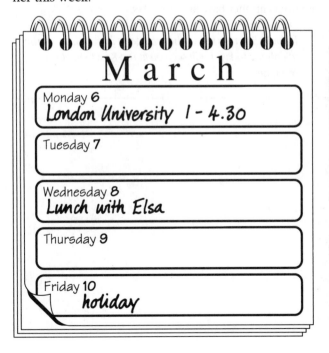

March

Monday **6**
London University 1 - 4.30

Tuesday **7**

Wednesday **8**
Lunch with Elsa

Thursday **9**

Friday **10**
holiday

Call 2 Receive the call.

It is Monday 16 June. You are Kate Palmer, technical advisor at MA Electronics.

JUNE

4
Monday — *lunch - Klaus + Anna*

5
Tuesday — *meeting with Mayor 2pm*

6
Wednesday — *Franco Rossi 11am*

7
Thursday

8
Friday — *Glasgow trade fair*

© Macmillan Publishers Limited 1995.

Making an appointment Worksheet 16b

NOTE: This activity is not linked to the activity on Worksheet 16a.

ACTIVITY
Pairwork: speaking

AIM
To make, change and cancel appointments on the telephone.

GRAMMAR AND FUNCTIONS
Suggestions: *Would you like to…? How about…?*
   Could you…?
Refusing and accepting

VOCABULARY
Appointments: *to make/cancel an appointment, to arrange, to have a meeting*
Prepositions of place: *at a conference/trade fair, in Belgium/Paris, on holiday, at the office*

PREPARATION
Make one copy of the worksheet for each pair of students in the class. Cut out Student A and Student B sections as indicated.

TIME
30 minutes

PROCEDURE

1 Ask students to work in pairs and divide them into Student A and Student B. Give each student the appropriate part of the worksheet.

2 Tell the students that they are going to make and receive two telephone calls according to the instructions on the worksheet.

3 Model the activity with a student.
   For example:
      You: *I need to see you. Can we meet tomorrow?* (shake your head to prompt the answer *No* from the student.)
      Student: *I'm sorry, I can't. I'm busy tomorrow.*
      You: *Oh. How about Friday?* (nod your head to prompt the answer *Yes* from the student).
      Student: *That sounds fine. What time?*
      You: *Let's meet at my office at 4 pm.*
      Student: *Okay, I'll see you there.*

4 Give the students a few minutes to study the diaries and the instructions on their worksheets.

5 Ask the students to work in pairs of one Student A and one Student B. Ask each pair to sit back-to-back so they cannot see each other, or see each other's worksheets.

6 When they are ready, the students make and receive their calls and write the arrangements in their diaries.

7 When they have finished, ask each pair of students to compare their diaries to check they have understood each other correctly.

FOLLOW-UP
Ask students to write a short fax confirming one of the arrangements they have just made. For example:
   Dear Charles,
   I would like to confirm the arrangement we made on the telephone today. I will see you at the Kowloon House restaurant on …

© Macmillan Publishers Limited 1995.

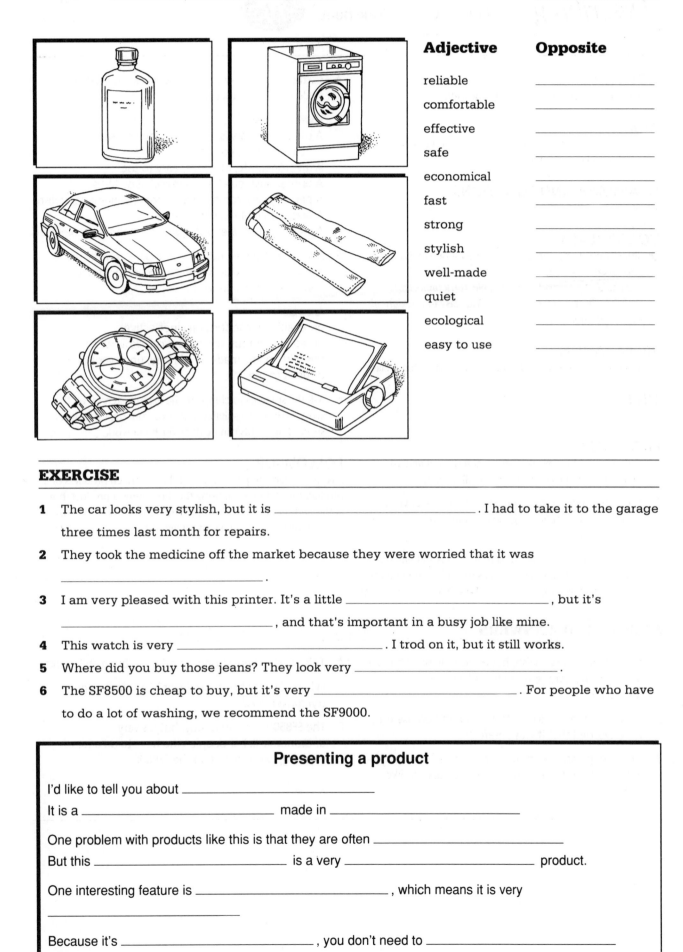

Adjective	Opposite
reliable	_____
comfortable	_____
effective	_____
safe	_____
economical	_____
fast	_____
strong	_____
stylish	_____
well-made	_____
quiet	_____
ecological	_____
easy to use	_____

EXERCISE

1 The car looks very stylish, but it is _____ . I had to take it to the garage three times last month for repairs.

2 They took the medicine off the market because they were worried that it was

_____ .

3 I am very pleased with this printer. It's a little _____ , but it's

_____ , and that's important in a busy job like mine.

4 This watch is very _____ . I trod on it, but it still works.

5 Where did you buy those jeans? They look very _____ .

6 The SF8500 is cheap to buy, but it's very _____ . For people who have to do a lot of washing, we recommend the SF9000.

Presenting a product

I'd like to tell you about _____

It is a _____ made in _____

One problem with products like this is that they are often _____

But this _____ is a very _____ product.

One interesting feature is _____ , which means it is very

_____

Because it's _____ , you don't need to _____

© Macmillan Publishers Limited 1995.

Describing a product Worksheet **17**

ACTIVITY
Pairwork or groupwork, classwork: speaking

AIM
To apply adjectives to different products to describe their advantages and disadvantages.

GRAMMAR AND FUNCTIONS
To be and *to look*

VOCABULARY
Qualities of products: *(un)ecological, fast/slow, quiet/noisy, (in)effective, strong/weak, safe/dangerous, well-made/badly-made, (un)reliable, (un)comfortable, stylish/ugly or plain, (un)economical, easy to use/difficult or complicated to use*

PREPARATION
Make one copy of the worksheet for each student in the class.

TIME
35 minutes

PROCEDURE
1 Give a copy of the worksheet to each student and ask them to name the products that are illustrated.

2 Focus the students' attention on the list of adjectives and go through them, checking their meaning and pronunciation.

3 Ask the students to work in pairs or groups and find three adjectives which describe qualities that it is important for each product to have.

4 Go through the answers with the whole class, asking the students to justify each answer.

Possible answers
A car: reliable, stylish, fast, economical, safe, comfortable, ecological
A medicine: safe, effective, easy to use
A printer: fast, quiet, economical, easy to use
A pair of jeans: comfortable, strong, well-made, stylish
A watch: reliable, stylish, strong
A washing machine: fast, quiet, economical, ecological

5 Ask the students, in their pairs or groups, to write the opposites of the adjectives and to record the correct answers on the worksheet.

Answers
unreliable, uncomfortable, ineffective, unsafe/dangerous, uneconomical, slow, weak, unstylish, badly-made, loud/noisy, unecological, difficult to use

6 Ask the students to complete the gap-fill exercise on the worksheet with a suitable adjective from the list. If you are short of time, this can be done for homework.

FOLLOW-UP
Ask the students to present one of the illustrated products or a product they know well, using the 'Presenting a product' box at the bottom of the worksheet to help them. They should say what its advantages and disadvantages are.

SUGGESTED ANSWERS

1 The car looks very stylish, but it is unreliable. I had to take it to the garage three times last month for repairs.

2 They took the medicine off the market because they were worried that it was unsafe.

3 I am very pleased with this printer. It's a little noisy, but it's fast and that's important in a busy job like mine.

4 This watch is very strong. I trod on it, but it still works.

5 Where did you buy those jeans? They look very stylish/well-made.

6 The SF8500 is cheap to buy, but it's very uneconomical. For people who have to do a lot of washing, we recommend the SF9000.

© Macmillan Publishers Limited 1995.

18 | *Which car?*

Unicello is a company based in Italy which sells mobile telephones. Its sales reps travel all over southern Europe by car. It is three years since the company last bought cars for the sales team and it now wants to buy a new type of car. There is a choice of three cars: the Lynx 320 SX, the Commodore 200Si, or the Toida Dart.

Student A

Lynx 320 SX

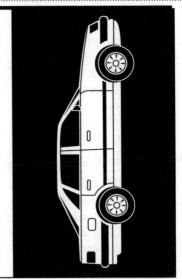

	Lynx 320 SX	Commodore 200Si	Toida Dart
Carphone included	Yes		
Airbag	Yes		
Engine size	2.0l		
Alarm	Yes		
Catalytic converter	No		
Power steering	Yes		
Comfort	Good		
Fuel economy	Good		
Insurance group (1–20)	10		
Price	$22,000		

Student B

Commodore 200SI

	Lynx 320 SX	Commodore 200Si	Toida Dart
Carphone included		No	
Airbag		Yes	
Engine size		2.5l	
Alarm		Yes	
Catalytic converter		No	
Power steering		Yes	
Comfort		Excellent	
Fuel economy		Average	
Insurance group (1–20)		16	
Price		$28,000	

Student C

Toida Dart

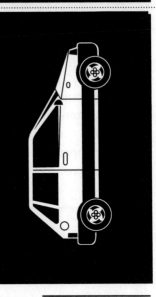

	Lynx 320 SX	Commodore 200Si	Toida Dart
Carphone included			No
Airbag			Yes
Engine size			1.7l
Alarm			No
Catalytic converter			Yes
Power steering			No
Comfort			Good
Fuel economy			Very good
Insurance group (1–20)			8
Price			$21,500

© Macmillan Publishers Limited 1995.

PHOTOCOPIABLE

Which car? Worksheet 18

ACTIVITY
Groupwork: speaking

AIM
To compare the features and performance of three products (cars) and choose the best.

GRAMMAR AND FUNCTIONS
Comparative and superlative adjectives: *-er, -est, more than, the most*
Have got and *there is/are*
Question words
How much? How many?

VOCABULARY
Adjectives: *comfortable, expensive, cheap, economical, good, bad (better, worse), high, low*
Features of a car: *alarm, carphone, airbag, power steering, catalytic converter*

PREPARATION
Make one copy of the text at the top of the worksheet for each student in the class. Cut out the sections as indicated and divide equally between groups of three students.

TIME
30 minutes

PROCEDURE
1 Elicit from the students features of a car that determine a) its economy, b) its comfort, c) its environmental friendliness, and d) its safety.

2 Give each student a copy of the text at the top of the worksheet and ask them to read it. Tell them that they are going to choose a car for the company's salespeople.

3 Discuss with the whole class what qualities are going to be important.

4 Ask the students to work in groups of three, Student A, Student B and Student C. Give each student the appropriate part of the worksheet.

5 Tell the students that they have information on one of the cars. Explain that they must ask and answer questions about the features of the other two cars with other students in their group. As they do this, they should fill in the table.

6 When they have finished, ask the groups to make comparisons between the three cars.
For example:
    The Toida Dart is the most economical.
    The Lynx is a little more expensive than the Toida Dart.

7 Ask students to choose which one is best for the company to buy and then to report their decision to the rest of the class, giving reasons for their choice.

PAIRWORK OPTION
Use only the Student A and Student B parts of the worksheet and ask the students to compare and then choose between these two cars (the Lynx and the Commodore 200Si).

FOLLOW-UP
Either ask students to talk about and compare rival products in a market they know well, or ask them to comment on these three types of company and say which they would prefer: a large multinational, a small family business, a charity.

ANSWERS

	Lynx 320 SX	Commodore 200Si	Toida Dart
Carphone included	Yes	No	No
Airbag	Yes	Yes	Yes
Engine size	2.0l	2.5l	1.7l
Alarm	Yes	Yes	No
Catalytic converter	No	No	Yes
Power steering	Yes	Yes	No
Comfort	Good	Excellent	Good
Fuel economy	Good	Average	Very good
Insurance group (1–20)	10	16	8
Price	$22,000	$28,000	$21,500

© Macmillan Publishers Limited 1995.

■ **Credit (general loans)**
■ **Insurance**
■ **Tipping**
■ **Tax**
■ **Payment**
■ **Attitude to money**
■ **Mortgages (house loans)**

A

Credit is quite easy. Many people buy things like TVs, washing machines and cars on credit. They pay a small deposit and then make monthly payments over two or three years. But interest rates are high: 20–30% a year. Banks offer many different types of loans, but there are also many small finance companies who want to give personal loans. Buying a house is not difficult either. Banks and building societies will lend you up to three and half times your annual salary. This is often as much as 95% of the cost of the house.

B

Generally, we are not a country which uses cash very much. Payment by credit card is becoming more usual now, but a lot of people still use their cheque books to pay for everything, even when the amount is small. You need to have a special cheque guarantee card, since people in Britain do not carry identity cards.

For services such as gas, telephone, electricity, water or other regular payments (insurance, loans, etc) people find it easier to pay by direct debit.

C

People don't like to talk about salaries or income. But they are very happy to tell you how much their new jacket cost in the sales, or what they saved on their new cooker. Bargaining in shops is not usual, but when you buy something second-hand, it's OK to discuss the price.

Generally, people do not carry much cash and we don't leave tips for bar staff, cinema staff, or even waiters when the service is included in the bill.

D

Income tax is quite low in Britain, with a top rate of 40% and a bottom rate of 20%. Most people pay about 25%. For employees of companies, this is taken out of their monthly salaries, before they receive their pay cheque. We also pay 10% National Insurance for social security benefits, like pensions, health and unemployment. The problem is that we have a lot of other taxes, some direct, like local government tax, and some indirect, like VAT, a consumer tax of 17.5% on almost all goods and services.

© Macmillan Publishers Limited 1995.

Money matters **Worksheet** *19*

ACTIVITY
Pairwork and whole class: reading, speaking

AIM
To talk about the way money is used: systems of payment, borrowing and tax.

GRAMMAR AND FUNCTIONS
Making comparisons and talking about similarities and differences: *the same as, different from, more than, less than*

VOCABULARY
Money: *payment, credit, debit, tax, interest, social security benefit, insurance, an amount, a loan, a cheque, cash, a tip, a bill, a rate, to bargain, to save, to lend, annual, monthly, direct, second-hand*

PREPARATION
Make one copy of the worksheet for each student.

TIME
40 to 60 minutes

PROCEDURE
1   Ask the students to think of all the things that you can do with money, for example, s*pend it, save it, borrow it, pay with it.*

2   Give a copy of the worksheet to each student and go through the table at the top, checking that they know the terms.

3   Ask students to read the texts and to match the letters A, B, C, D to the corresponding headings at the top of the page. (Each text may correspond to more than one heading.)

4   Ask students to check their answers in pairs.

5   Check again with the whole class and ask one or two students to describe the characteristics of one of the financial practices in Britain.

6   Allocate a particular area, such as *tipping* or *tax*, to a pair of students and ask them to make comparisons between the British system and financial practices in their own countries.
    For example:
    We have the same attitude to tipping as the British.
    The rate of income tax is higher than in Britain.
    It's more difficult to buy a house.

7   Each pair should then report back to the rest of the class.

FOLLOW-UP
Ask the students to write a letter of advice to someone who is coming to live in their country. For example:
    Always give a tip to the barman.
    Don't carry a lot of cash with you.

ANSWERS

Credit (general loans)	A
Insurance	D
Tipping	C
Tax	D
Payment	B
Attitude to money	C and B
Mortgages (house loans)	A

© Macmillan Publishers Limited 1995.

A

Make enquiries

1 You'd like to take some clients out to dinner. Ask the hotel receptionist to recommend a good restaurant. Find out the distance and how to get there.

2 You are in New York. You want to get to Chicago as quickly as possible. Ask the hotel travel agent about the type of transport, cost and time of the journey.

3 Your suit needs to be dry cleaned. Ask at hotel reception if they can do it.

4 You'd like to go on an excursion this weekend. Ask the hotel receptionist what trips they have, the cost and the time of each.

Information

Translation services

Ready in 24 hours (for less than 10 pages) $15 per page

Delivery services to Union City – 40 kilometres

Gold Star	2 hours	$24 (less than 5 kg)	$32 (less than 10 kg)
Silver Service	same day	$16 (less than 7 kg)	$22 (less than 12 kg)

SHOPS

Macey's
  department store
  3 kilometres
  5 minutes by taxi
Charles Church
  gift shop
  1 kilometre
  10 minutes walk
CHL department
  department store
  5 kilometres
  15 minutes by subway or taxi

New York–Philadelphia

Distance:	130 kilometres
Type of road:	Freeway (speed limit 90 kph)
Time:	2 hours

B

Make enquiries

1 You are going to give a presentation, but your diagrams (8 of them) are in French. You would like someone to translate them and print them in English. Ask a secretary about translation services: the cost and the time.

2 You want to send some technical data to a factory in Union City to arrive as quickly as possible. The weight of the parcel is 6 kg. Ask a secretary about delivery services: the cost and the time.

3 You would like to buy a present for a client. Ask a secretary about shops: the kind, the distance and the time it takes to get there.

4 You want to drive to Philadelphia tomorrow, because you have a meeting there. Ask a secretary about the distance and the time it takes to get there.

Information

RESTAURANT GUIDE

Rating: * = poor ***** = excellent

Giovanni's Restaurant	Italian	1 km (10 minutes walk) ***
Le Manoir de New York	French	6 km (15 minutes by taxi) ****
Brown's Restaurant	International	0.5 km (5 minutes walk) ***

DRY CLEANING

	Regular service (next day)	Gold star service (4 hours)
Trousers/skirts	$4.50	$6
Overcoats	$8	$11.50
Suits (2 piece)	$12	$18

New York–Chicago

Plane
  2 hours
    $145 one way
    ($235 round trip)
    Every hour

Train
  5 hours
    $84 round trip
    Every two hours

Hire car
  6 hours
    $48 per day

Excursions

Manhattan from the air
half a day   the world's most famous skyscrapers – by helicopter
$108

Statue of Liberty
half a day   the world's most famous monument – by boat
$28

Washington DC
two days   the home of the US Government – by bus
$130

© Macmillan Publishers Limited 1995.

How long does it take? Worksheet 20

ACTIVITY
Pairwork, groupwork: speaking

AIM
To ask about time, distance and cost.

GRAMMAR AND FUNCTIONS
Question forms with *How: How far is it? How long does it take? How much does it cost?*
What kind of...?

VOCABULARY
Travel: *to recommend, to translate, an excursion, a department store, one way, round trip, by coach/boat/helicopter etc, a parcel, data, a delivery service*

PREPARATION
Make one copy of the worksheet for each pair of students in the class. Cut out Student A and Student B sections as indicated.

TIME
30 minutes

PROCEDURE
1 Explain to the students that they are on a business trip and they have a number of different things they need to do. Student A will ask staff in a hotel for some information and Student B will ask a secretary.

2 Ask the students to work in pairs and divide them into Student A and Student B. Give each student the appropriate part of the worksheet.

3 Give the students a few minutes to study their worksheet.

4 Ask Student As to look at the 'Make enquiries' section on their worksheets and Student Bs to look at the 'Information' section.

5 Model the activity taking the part of Student A yourself. Choose a confident Student B to work with you.
For example:
　　You: *Excuse me?*
　　Student B: *Can I help you?*
　　You: *Can you recommend a good restaurant for dinner?*
　　Student: *Well, Le Manoir de New York, is very nice.*
　　You: *How far is it from the hotel?*
　　Student B: *It's 6 km.*
　　You: *And how should I get there?*
　　Student B: *It's only 15 minutes by taxi.*

6 Ask the students, in pairs, to act out the dialogues, taking it in turns to make and answer enquiries.

7 Ask the students to think of one more exchange between visitor and receptionist or secretary, and then ask them to act this out in front of the class.

© Macmillan Publishers Limited 1995.

16-20 | *Crossword*

Student A

CLUES ACROSS

1 People can only *borrow* money if they give the bank some guarantee that they can pay it back.

4 _____

_____

6 _____

_____

7 _____

_____

11 _____

_____

14 _____

_____

15 _____

_____

16 _____

_____

¹B	O	²R	O	W		³	
				⁴C	A	S	⁵H
		⁶T	A	X			
⁷S	⁸A	L	E				
				⁹			
						¹⁰	
¹¹M	¹²O	¹³N	T	H	L	Y	
			¹⁴L	E	N	D	S
		¹⁵C	O	S	T	¹⁶T	O

Student B

CLUES DOWN

1 He *buys* a new car every two years.

2 _____

3 _____

_____

5 _____

_____

8 _____

_____

9 _____

_____

10 _____

_____

12 _____

_____

13 _____

_____

¹B		²R			³S		
U		A		⁴A		⁵H	
Y		⁶T			A	I	
⁷S	⁸L	E			E	G	
	O			⁹P		H	
	A			A	¹⁰C		
¹¹	¹²O	¹³N	T	Y	R		
F		I		M	E		
F		P	¹⁴	E	D		
E				N	I		
R		¹⁵		T	¹⁶T		

© Macmillan Publishers Limited 1995.

PHOTOCOPIABLE

Crossword Worksheet Progress check 16–20

ACTIVITY
Pairwork: reading, speaking

AIM
To write clues for a crossword and to complete it.

VOCABULARY
Money: *payment, credit, a loan, cash, rate, to borrow, to save, to lend, monthly, high, to cost, to offer, tax, sale*

PREPARATION
Make one copy of the worksheet for each pair of students in the class. Cut out the two crosswords as indicated.

TIME
30 minutes

PROCEDURE
1   Tell the students that they are going to do a crossword, but that they are going to write some of the clues themselves.

2   Divide the class into two groups of Student As and Student Bs. Ask the students to work with a partner from the same group. Give each student the appropriate crossword.

3   Ask the students to look at the words which are written on their crossword.

4   Explain that they must write clues for these words. Write this sentence on the board. For example:
    That washing machine is expensive to buy, but _____ to run. Elicit the word *cheap*.
    Check the students have understood exactly what they have to do.

5   When they have prepared their clues, put the students into new pairs of one Student A and one Student B.

6   When they are ready, ask the students to take it in turns to read their clues to each other in order to complete the crossword. They must not show their worksheet to the other student.

7   Check the answers with the whole class.

OPTION
If you prefer a simpler and quicker way, give the students the clues below for them to read to the other student.

Clues for Student A
Across
1   People can only _____ money if they give the bank some guarantee that they can pay it back.
4   How would you like to pay? In _____ or by credit card?
6   Many governments put a _____ of about 15% on all goods; on cigarettes and alcohol it can be much higher.
7   If you want to pay less for goods it's better to wait until the shop has a _____ .
11 Most employees receive a _____ pay cheque, but a few are paid each week.
14 & 16 The Commercial Bank _____ $30 million a year _____ small businesses.
15 How much does it _____ to rent a small flat in the centre of Paris?
16 See 14.

Clues for Student B
Down
1   He _____ a new car every two years.
2   The interest _____ is better if you invest more than £10,000.
3   You can _____ money if you buy goods in bulk.
5   We decided to borrow the money from the finance company, because the interest rate was not as _____ as at the bank.
8   We asked the bank for a _____ to pay for the new machines.
9   The company expects _____ for all goods within 30 days.
10 The company offers _____ to customers who do not want to pay the full amount immediately.
12 We _____ a 20% discount on all orders which are more than $1000.
13 Is service included or do we need to leave a _____ for the waiter?

Answers

¹B	O	R	²R	O	W		³S				
U			A			⁴C	A	⁵S	H		
Y		⁶T	A	X		V		I			
⁷S	A	L	E			E		G			
	O				⁹P			H			
	A				A		¹⁰C				
¹¹M	¹²O	N	¹³T	H	L	Y	R				
	F		I		M		E				
	F		P	¹⁴L	E	N	D	S			
	E		N		N		I				
	R		¹⁵C	O	S	T	¹⁶T	O			

© Macmillan Publishers Limited 1995.

Recruitment details

Technical Consultant

(Southern and Eastern Africa)

SALARY £30,000 + 2-year contract

Onito Limited is a company with 25 years' experience in consultancy
and training. We provide technical assistance for projects in developing
countries.

We are looking for someone to manage environmental projects in
South and East Africa: nature conservation, water management,
pollution control and agricultural development.

You will be responsible for administration and financial control and will
have to work with government departments in each country.
We would like to hear from people with suitable work experience and an
interest in development aid. Good written and spoken English is
important and knowledge of the area is an advantage.

ONITO

	CANDIDATE 1 *Greg Harris*	CANDIDATE 2 *Lisa Simpson*
Personal details (marital status, age, languages spoken, interests)		
Education		
Qualifications		
Experience of other countries		
Work experience		

© Macmillan Publishers Limited 1995.

PHOTOCOPIABLE

Choosing the right candidate Worksheets  **21a** and **21b**

NOTE: Use Worksheets 21a and 21b for this activity.

ACTIVITY
Pairwork: reading, speaking

AIM
To ask and answer questions about someone's education, qualifications and work experience.

GRAMMAR AND FUNCTIONS
Talking about experiences
Present perfect simple contrasted with past simple

VOCABULARY
Job advertisements: *suitable, experience, a qualification, CV, an advantage, to provide, knowledge*
Development: *environment, conservation, pollution, farmer, agriculture, developing, aid project*

PREPARATION
Make one copy of the top section of Worksheet 21a (recruitment details) for each student . Make one copy of the bottom section of Worksheet 21a (recruitment details) for half the class (interviewers). Make one copy of Worksheet 21b (CVs) for the other half of the class (interviewees). Cut out the Student A and Student B sections as indicated.

TIME
30 minutes

PROCEDURE
1 Tell the students that they are going to look at a job advertisement and that half the class will be interviewers and the other half interviewees.

2 Give the students a copy of the top section of Worksheet 21a and ask them to find out what the job is and what qualifications are needed for it. Discuss the answers with the whole class.

3 Divide the class into two groups: interviewers and interviewees.

4 Divide the interviewees into Student As and Student Bs and give them the appropriate CV on Worksheet 21b. Ask them to read their CV and to think about why they are applying for the advertised job.

5 Put the interviewers into pairs and ask them to study the table on the bottom of Worksheet 21a and prepare the questions they are going to ask.

6 When they are ready, either ask each interviewer to interview one candidate, or ask the two interviewers to interview the candidates in turn, one after the other.

7 The two interviewers should now decide on which of the two candidates is most suitable for the job.

8 Ask students to report back to the class, giving reasons for their choice.

FOLLOW-UP
Ask the interviewers to write a short memo to their managing director explaining who they have chosen for the job and why. Ask the interviewees to write a letter of acceptance for the job.

© Macmillan Publishers Limited 1995.

Student A

CURRICULUM VITAE

Name	Greg Harris	Date of Birth	28/5/66
Nationality	Australian	Marital Status	Married

Education and Qualifications
1984–88	University of Melbourne	BSc in Environmental Studies
1989–90	Agricultural College of Santiago, Chile	MSc in Agricultural Science

Work Experience
1988–89	Voluntary Service Overseas (VSO)	Research assistant on water pollution study in Brazil.
1991–93	Ministry of Agriculture, Egypt	Assistant to Head of 'Clean Water Project'.
1993–present	JM Hopper Farms, Kansas, USA	Working as an agricultural consultant for a large private farm.

Languages
English	Good spoken and written
Portuguese	OK for everyday conversation

Interests
Sports, cinema and theatre

Student B

CURRICULUM VITAE

Name Lisa Simpson		**Date of Birth** 22/1/60	
Nationality American		**Marital Status** Single	

Education and Qualifications
1978–85	Stanford University, California	PhD in Agricultural Economics

Work Experience
1985–86	Stanford University	Assistant Lecturer in Department of Human Sciences
1986–89	Columbia University, New York	Lecturer in Agricultural Economics
1989–92	Center for Policy Studies, Mexico	Advisor to Mexican Department of Agriculture
1992–present	Overseas Development Organisation	Press Officer in New York office

Languages
English Fluent   Spanish Fluent

Interests
Politics, travel, reading and walking

© Macmillan Publishers Limited 1995.

PHOTOCOPIABLE

Student A

Government action – *but what has been the result?*

- ☐ They have employed more police officers.

- ☐ They have opened training centres for people who are unemployed.

- ☐ They have introduced a system of student grants.

- ☐ They have privatized the national electricity company.

- ☐ They have improved the railway system.

- ☐ They have opened many new nursery schools.

- ☐ They have spent a lot of money on cleaning up beaches and the countryside.

- ☐ They have run a national campaign on health education.

✂ ·······

Student B

Result – *but how have they managed to do it?*

- ☐ They have reduced the number of cars on the roads.

- ☐ They have encouraged more tourists to visit the country.

- ☐ Crime has gone down.

- ☐ In the last two years more people have attended university than ever before.

- ☐ Electricity prices have fallen.

- ☐ More women have been able to go out to work.

- ☐ They have reduced the number of working days lost through sickness.

- ☐ Unemployment has gone down.

© Macmillan Publishers Limited 1995.

PHOTOCOPIABLE

Government measures Worksheet 22a

NOTE: This activity is not linked to the activity on Worksheet 22b.

ACTIVITY
Pairwork: speaking

AIM
To talk about recent actions and their results.

GRAMMAR AND FUNCTIONS
Present perfect simple for past actions with present results

VOCABULARY
The economy: *unemployment, interest rates, inflation, a tourist, a grant, to spend money on, to raise money, to run a campaign, to encourage, to reduce, to privatise, to improve*

PREPARATION
Make one copy of the worksheet for each pair of students in the class. Cut out the Student A and Student B sections as indicated.

TIME
25 minutes

PROCEDURE
1 Ask the students where government money comes from and elicit *taxes, borrowing* and *privatization*. Then ask where it goes to elicit *health, education, defence, social security*.

2 Tell them that they are going to find out what the government has done recently and whether these measures have been successful.

3 Ask students to work in pairs and divide them into Student A and Student B. Give each student a copy of the appropriate part of the worksheet.

4 Ask students to read the information on their worksheet for a moment.

5 Ask Student A to begin by telling Student B one of the things that the government has done and to ask Student B what the result has been. Student B must choose the result which fits the action and reply to Student A.

6 Now it is Student B's turn to tell Student A one of the results and ask Student A how the government has managed to do this. Student A must choose the action which fits the result and reply to Student B.

7 Ask the students to think of actions that their government has done recently and/or things that it has achieved. They should then present these to the rest of the class. For example:
   a *Our government has introduced a new tax on cars.*
   b *Our government has improved the education system.*

In statements like *a*, the other students should ask questions to find out the result.

In statements like *b*, the other students should ask questions to find out how it managed to achieve this.

FOLLOW-UP
Ask the students to write a short report on a successful government measure.

ANSWERS

They have employed more police officers. Crime has gone down.

They have opened training centres for people who are unemployed. Unemployment has gone down.

They have introduced a system of student grants. In the last two years more people have attended university than ever before.

They have privatised the national electricity company. Electricity prices have fallen.

They have improved the railway system. They have reduced the number of cars on the roads.

They have opened many new nursery schools. More women have been able to go out to work.

They have spent a lot of money on cleaning up beaches and the countryside. They have encouraged more tourists to visit the country.

They have run a national campaign on health education. They have reduced the number of working days lost through sickness.

© Macmillan Publishers Limited 1995.

You are the new assistant manager at the Regency Hotel, a small family hotel.
When you arrive at the hotel, you find that many things are wrong, and you want to
discuss them with the manager.

Problem	Action taken
Many employees only stay for three or four months. Training new people is expensive.	
The restaurant is losing money because hotel guests prefer to visit other restaurants in the town. 	
Not many guests visit the hotel in the winter.	
Guests have complained about mistakes in their bills.	
It is difficult for guests to park their cars near the hotel.	
Not many guests come from abroad.	

© Macmillan Publishers Limited 1995.

PHOTOCOPIABLE

Problem solving **Worksheet** *22b*

NOTE: This activity is not linked with the activity on Worksheet 22a.

ACTIVITY
Pairwork: speaking

AIM
To think of solutions to problems and then to report on action taken.

GRAMMAR AND FUNCTIONS
Present perfect simple for describing recent actions

VOCABULARY
Hotels: *bill, guest, complain, mistake, training, abroad*

PREPARATION
Make one copy of the worksheet for each student in the class.

TIME
25 minutes

PROCEDURE

1 Give a worksheet to each student and ask them to read the information at the top. Explain that they are going to have to solve some problems that this hotel is facing.

2 Go through the problems, checking that the students understand each one.

3 Ask students to work in pairs or groups of three to think of a solution for each problem.

4 When they have finished, each pair or group should report back to the class on the action they have taken to solve each problem.

5 Conduct a class discussion on the best solution to each problem.

6 If you like, ask each pair or group to think of another problem the hotel is facing to present to the rest of the class to solve.

FOLLOW-UP
Ask the students to write a short memo to their head office describing a recent problem (real or imaginary) in a company and saying what they have done about it.

© Macmillan Publishers Limited 1995.

Germany/be/one country again _____

The European Community/exist _____

May 1/be/an international public holiday _____

Coca Cola/be/in business _____

MS-DOS/be/the standard computer operating system _____

The USA/have/a space programme _____

There/be/a world-wide ban on nuclear testing _____

OPEC/control/the world price of oil _____

| for several years | since 1990 | for over 100 years | for about 40 years |
| since the war | since 1980 | since 1920 | since the early 1970s |

- - - - - - fold -

How long has your country existed? _____
* * *

How long have you had the system of government that you have today? _____
* * *

How long has the present government in your country been in power? _____
* * *

What traditional product or service does your country export and how long has it
exported this? _____
* * *

How long has your company been in business? _____
* * *

What is its newest product and how long has it been on the market? _____
* * *

How long have you worked for your company? _____
* * *

How long have you had your present job? _____

© Macmillan Publishers Limited 1995.

PHOTOCOPIABLE

Business history   Worksheet   23

ACTIVITY
Pairwork: speaking

AIM
To talk about how long certain things have been established.

GRAMMAR AND FUNCTIONS
For and *since* with present perfect simple

VOCABULARY
General: *the European Community, a public holiday, computer operating system, space programme, nuclear testing, world-wide, to be in power*

PREPARATION
Make one copy of the worksheet for each student, and fold the worksheet as indicated.

TIME
15 minutes

PROCEDURE

1 Tell the students that they are going to decide when certain important business and political events happened.

2 Give one copy of the folded worksheet to each student and ask them to look at the top section. Ask them to work in pairs to match the dates in the box to the events. Encourage them to put sentences into the correct tense. For example:

> *I think May 1 has been a public holiday for nearly a 100 years.*

If students have difficulty forming the present perfect from the prompts, ask them to write their answers in the space provided.

3 Check the answers with the whole class by asking students to read out their sentences.

4 Ask the students to unfold the worksheet and look at the questions. Ask the students to work in pairs to ask and answer the questions, making a note of their partner's answers.

5 Ask the students to report back their findings to the whole class. Is there any information they find particularly interesting or surprising?

ANSWERS

Germany has been one country again since 1990.

The European Community has existed for about 40 years.

May 1 has been an international public holiday for over 100 years.

Coca-Cola has been in business since 1920.

MS-DOS has been the standard computer operating system since 1980.

The USA has had a space programme since the war.

There has been a world-wide ban on nuclear testing for several years.

OPEC has controlled the world price of oil since the early 1970s.

© Macmillan Publishers Limited 1995.

Student A

> How do you pronounce *subsidiary*?

> What does *launch* mean?

> What's the word for a person who sells things for a company?

> What's the word for the things which people buy on the stock market?

> How do you spell that?

Find out the word – ask questions.

1 It's a building. You store goods in it.
2 It's a person. He or she looks after the financial records of a company.
3 It's a diagram. It uses lines to show the performance of a company.
4 It's part of a building. You receive visitors there.
5 They are people. They do not work all the time for the company.
6 It's a department. It deals with training, welfare, salaries and pensions.

Explain the word – give answers.

supplier	turnover	invoice	agent	brochure	consumer

Student B

> How do you pronounce *subsidiary*?

> What does *launch* mean?

> What's the word for a person who sells things for a company?

> What's the word for the things which people buy on the stock market?

> How do you spell that?

Find out the word – ask questions.

1 It's all the money. It comes into the company from sales of its products.
2 It's a person. He or she uses goods.
3 It's a document. It tells people about a company's products.
4 It's a company. It provides your company with the things it needs.
5 It's a piece of paper. It tells you how much you have to pay for goods.
6 It's a person. He or she represents your company in another country.

Explain the word – give answers.

part-time staff	personnel	reception	warehouse	accountant	graph

© Macmillan Publishers Limited 1995.

ACTIVITY
Pairwork: speaking

AIM
To give definitions of words and to learn new words their meaning, pronunciation and spelling.

GRAMMAR AND FUNCTIONS
Defining relative clauses using *who, which, where*
Learning new words

VOCABULARY
Company terms: *an agent, turnover (financial), a supplier, a subsidiary, a warehouse, a salesman, an accountant, part-time, personnel, an invoice, reception*

PREPARATION
Make one copy of the worksheet for each pair of students in the class. Cut out Student A and Student B sections as indicated.

TIME
40 minutes

PROCEDURE
1   Ask the students to work in pairs and divide the class into Student A and Student B. Give each student the appropriate part of the worksheet.

2   Ask the students to look at the speech bubbles at the top of their worksheet. Explain that they must ask and answer the questions in the speech bubbles with their partner.

3   Check the answers with the whole class.

4   Tell them that they are going to try to find the right word for something by asking questions.

Write on the board:
   They are people. They buy things from a company.
Elicit or give students the question:
   What is the word for people who buy things from a company?

5   Draw students' attention to the 'Find out the word' section on their worksheets and explain that they must make questions from these sentences.

6   Explain that the student who is asked the question must then choose the correct word from the list of words under the 'Explain the word' section.
The student who asked the question should also be encouraged to ask about the spelling and pronunciation of the word.
For example:
   How do you spell that? How do you pronounce that?

7   Explain that they can either ask and answer questions alternately, or Student A can ask all his/her questions and then Student B can do the same.

8   Check the answers and the pronunciation of each word with the whole class.

9   Ask each student to think of another thing they would like to know the name of, and then to put their question to the whole class.

FOLLOW-UP
Ask the students to choose from the words below and write suitable definitions. All these words will be used in the activities on the following worksheet.
   to fit, to attach, to switch on, a battery, solar power, packaging, waterproof

ANSWERS

Student A

1   warehouse
2   accountant
3   graph
4   reception
5   part-time staff
6   personnel

Student B

1   turnover
2   consumer
3   brochure
4   supplier
5   invoice
6   agent

© Macmillan Publishers Limited 1995.

EXPLORER'S HELMET

If you are going on safari or to visit the Pyramids in Egypt, this hat is for you. It has a small motor and fan which cools your forehead. The motor runs on solar power, so you don't need any batteries.

ZIP-IT-OPEN

You will never again cut your tongue or break your fingernails trying to open a plastic bag or plastic packaging. Zip-it-open can open almost any bag. It's safe and it fits in your pocket, so you can use it anywhere!

THE CEILING CLOCK

If you have to feed a baby in the middle of the night or take medicine at a particular time, then you need this clock. At night, using a light, it projects the time onto the ceiling in large numbers. You can read the time without getting out of bed, or switching on the light and waking up other people.

THE PLATEMATE

You are at a party. You meet someone and want to shake their hand. But you are holding a glass in one hand and a plate in the other. What do you do? Answer: you take your Platemate out of your pocket and attach it to your plate. Now just put the glass into the holder and one hand will be free.

THE SHOWER PHONE

What do you do when you are in the shower and the telephone starts ringing? Easy: you press the answer button on your Shower Phone and talk. It attaches to the wall and it is completely waterproof. Your hands are free to continue washing, while you make those important business or personal calls. You'll never have to miss a call again.

THE KEY-FINDER

Do you always lose your keys? Some people spend as much as half an hour each day looking for their keys. Relax. Key-finder is a small electronic device which attaches to your key ring. If you can't find your keys, make a loud noise and key finder will 'answer' with a loud bleep.

© Macmillan Publishers Limited 1995.

PHOTOCOPIABLE

Patent pending **Worksheet** 25

ACTIVITY
Groupwork: speaking

AIM
To describe things and what they do, or what they are used for.

GRAMMAR AND FUNCTIONS
Talking about function and purpose:
> It's a thing for...-ing
> You use it to...
> It's a thing you use to... (without) -ing

VOCABULARY
Gadgets: *to fit, to run on, to attach, to switch on, to project, a motor, a fan, a battery, solar power, packaging, a pocket, a device, a bleep, a holder, waterproof*
General: *to feed, fingernails*

PREPARATION
Make one copy of the worksheet for each group of four to six students in the class. Cut out the six sections as indicated.

TIME
25 minutes

PROCEDURE

1 Divide the class into groups of four to six students.

2 Introduce the idea of new and clever gadgets by drawing a diagram of this double umbrella on the board. Ask the students what it is and what it can be used for (it can be held by one person but keep two dry).
Elicit phrases:
> I think it's a thing for ...
> It's a thing you use for... -ing.
> No, actually it's a thing you use to...

Write the phrases on the board.

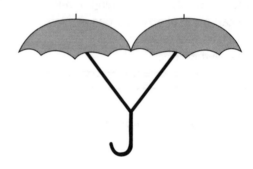

3 Tell the students that they are going to be given a description and a picture of a new gadget. The other students in the group must guess what it is and what it is used for.

4 Give a picture and description of one gadget to each member of the group. Ask them to read the information, but not to show the picture to anyone else in their group.

5 Ask students to fold their papers so that only the picture is visible and to show the picture to the other students in the group.

6 The others must try to deduce from the picture what the gadget is and what it is used for. Encourage the students to use the phrases on the board.

7 When they have finished trying to guess the purpose of the gadget, they should check with the student who has the information as to whether they are correct.

8 When the students have finished, discuss with the whole class which is the most useful gadget.

FOLLOW-UP
Ask the students to present gadgets/products of their own or to describe things that they have seen that have struck them as innovative and clever.

© Macmillan Publishers Limited 1995.

21-25 | *Success story*

Student A

As chairman of Microsoft Inc, Bill Gates is worth 2) $ _____ . He has lived and worked in Seattle since 3) _____
_____ .

Seattle was once famous for producing Boeing aircraft, but is now better known as the home of Microsoft. From his parents Bill got a good business sense and a quick mind (his mother was a 5) _____ , and his father was a lawyer).

He first became interested in computers when he was 7) _____ in Seattle. From there he went to Harvard University. He was a brilliant student. Most of the time he 10) _____ in the university laboratory. At the age of 19 he wrote 'Basic', the programming language which all early PCs used. He knew, even then, that he had the ability to revolutionize the world of computing and he left university before 12) _____ .

When he left Harvard he first worked for MITS, but a little while later he left and set up his own company, Microsoft.

In 1980, he bought a small company which produced 14) _____ .
Gates made some changes to it and renamed it MS-DOS. He sold the rights to use this system to IBM.
Since 17) _____ MS-DOS has been the standard operating system for almost all PCs. Microsoft has also developed well-known programs like 18) _____ and Excel. Some people say he wants complete control of the computer software market.

✂ -

Student B

As chairman of 1) _____ Inc, Bill Gates is worth $5 billion. He has lived and worked in Seattle since he was a boy. Seattle was once famous for producing 4) _____ , but it is now better known as the home of Microsoft. From his parents Bill got a good business sense and a quick mind (his mother was a company director, and his father was a 6) _____).

He first became interested in computers when he was at school in Seattle. From there he went to 8) _____
_____ . He was a 9) _____ student. Most of the time he worked on the computers in the university laboratory. At the age of 11) _____ , he wrote 'Basic', the programming language which all early PCs used. He knew, even then, that he had the ability to revolutionize the world of computing and he left university before finishing his studies.

When he left Harvard he first worked for 13) _____ , but a little while later he left and set up his own company, Microsoft.

In 1980, he bought a small company which produced an operating system called DOS. Gates made some changes to it and renamed it 15) _____ . He sold the rights to use this system to 16) _____ . Since 1980 MS-DOS has been the standard operating system for almost all PCs. Microsoft has also developed well-known programs like Windows and 19) _____ . Some people say he wants complete control of the computer software market.

© Macmillan Publishers Limited 1995.

PHOTOCOPIABLE

Success story Worksheet Progress check 21-25

ACTIVITY
Pairwork: reading, speaking

AIM
To talk about someone's career and achievements.

GRAMMAR AND FUNCTIONS
Present perfect simple and past simple

VOCABULARY
Computing: *a program, an operating system, a PC, software, the rights*

General: *to be worth, to inherit, to set up, to rename, to revolutionise, a rival, business sense, aggressive, ambitious*

PREPARATION
Make one copy of the worksheet for each pair of students in the class. Cut out the Student A and Student B sections as indicated.

TIME
30 minutes

PROCEDURE

1 Ask the students what they know about Bill Gates, the founder of Microsoft.
> *What field does he work in?*
> *What has he achieved?*
> *What kind of man is he?*

2 Divide the class equally into Student As and Student Bs. Give each student the appropriate part of the worksheet.

3 Explain to the students that they both have the same text with some information missing and that they are going to ask and answer questions to find the missing information.

4 Ask the students to read the text and to prepare the questions they will need to ask. They can do this part of the activity with someone from the same group or alone.

5 When they have done this, divide the class into pairs of one Student A with one Student B. They should take turns to question each other about the missing information, **beginning with Student B**. As they do so, they should fill in the gaps in the text.

6 Check the answers with the whole class and ask students to comment on what type of man Bill Gates is.

FOLLOW-UP
Ask the students to prepare a brief paragraph describing someone's career and achievements. They could choose their own if they like!

ANSWERS

As chairman of Microsoft Inc, Bill Gates is worth $5 billion. He has lived and worked in Seattle since he was a boy. Seattle was once famous for producing Boeing aircraft, but it is now better known as the home of Microsoft. From his parents, Bill got a good business sense and a quick mind, (his mother was a company director, and his father was a lawyer.)

He first became interested in computers when he was at school in Seattle. From there he went to Harvard University. He was a brilliant student. Most of the time he worked on the computers in the university laboratory. At the age of 19 he wrote 'Basic', the programming language which all early PCs used. He knew, even then, that he had the ability to revolutionize the world of computing and he left university before finishing his studies.

When he left Harvard he first worked for MITS, but a little while later he left and set up his own company, Microsoft.

In 1980, he bought a small company which produced an operating system called DOS. Gates made some changes to it and renamed it MS-DOS. He sold the rights to use this system to IBM. Since 1980 MS-DOS has been the standard operating system for almost all PCs. Microsoft has also developed well-known programs like Windows and Excel.

© Macmillan Publishers Limited 1995.

France Telecom
require a
Regional Sales Director (Far East Area)

The successful applicant must…

TV PRESENTER
required to present weekly business news programme for leading TV station

Applicants must…

- good knowledge of the Japanese distribution system
- contacts in political and business worlds
- between 35 and 45 years old
- five years experience in telecommunications
- at least two languages (one oriental)
- able to work under pressure
- a good record in selling
- good knowledge of world affairs
- a degree in Economics
- willing to travel
- smart appearance
- strong negotiating skills
- excellent presentation and communication skills

YOUR JOB

(company name) _____

require a (job title) _____

to (job description) _____

Applicants must be _____

and have _____

© Macmillan Publishers Limited 1995.

The right qualifications Worksheet 26

ACTIVITY
Pairwork: speaking

AIM
To talk about the requirements for a particular job:
personal qualities, skills and experience people must have.

GRAMMAR AND FUNCTIONS
Obligation, necessity and lack of necessity: *must, have to* and *don't have to/don't need to*

VOCABULARY
Qualifications and skills: *knowledge, experience, appearance, a contact, a record, a skill, a degree, to be willing, to work under pressure*

PREPARATION
Make one copy of the worksheet for each student in the class.

TIME
25 minutes

PROCEDURE

1 Ask students what kind of qualifications a bank manager should have.

2 Write up the two job titles, TV presenter and Regional Sales Manager, and ask the students what qualifications might be necessary for these jobs. Encourage them to use the target language.

3 Give the students a copy of the worksheet and ask them to work in pairs to say which qualifications on the list are necessary for each job.
For example:
> The sales director must have a good record in selling.
> The TV presenter doesn't need to have strong negotiating skills.

4 Go through the answers with the whole class. Below are suggested answers, but accept any reasonable answer.

5 Ask the students to look at the box marked 'Your job' at the bottom of the worksheet and write an advertisement for their own job or a job they would like to do. If you like, ask the other students to guess what qualifications are necessary for each job before the advertisement is presented to the class.

SUGGESTED ANSWERS

TV presenter
contacts in political and business worlds
between 35 and 45 years old
able to work under pressure
good knowledge of world affairs
a degree in Economics
excellent presentation and communication skills
smart appearance

Sales director
good knowledge of the Japanese distribution system
five years experience in telecommunications
at least two languages (one oriental)
a good record in selling
willing to travel
strong negotiating skills

© Macmillan Publishers Limited 1995.

Reward Pre-intermediate
Business Resource Pack

Student A **Student B**

John Coral and Partners

38 Marlborough Road
Swindon SW10 3PT

CCO Vending Machines
39 Charles Street
LONDON EC1 8BQ
12 March 1995

Dear Sir

I _____ your advertisement in *The Times* newspaper yesterday and I _____ some more information about your vending machines. We _____ our present machine for four years and need to replace it. _____ inform me about the price and the specifications of your ZX190?

I look forward to hearing from you.

Yours faithfully

Jefferson Sanders and Co. Chartered Accountants

78 Grays Road

LONDON N1 4PJ

12 March 1995
Rexa Window Locks
Unit 3B
Wilton Industrial Park
Swindon SW3 6AF

Dear Sir/Madam

We _____ some problems with security in our offices recently. It is an old building which has many large wooden windows. We _____ _____ some good window locks and a colleague _____ your company to me. _____ send me details of your product range and tell me if you have _____ .

I look forward to hearing from you.

Yours faithfully

Rexa Window Locks

- fits any type of window
- opens and locks easily
- no key necessary
- installation service
- comes with a 5 year guarantee

ZX190 Vending Machine (for hot and cold drinks)

- holds up to 100 cans
- accepts any coin
- gives change
- serves hot and cold drinks
- self-cleaning
- gives instructions in three languages

REXA WINDOW LOCKS

Unit 3B Wilton Industrial Park Swindon SW3 6AF

CCO VENDING MACHINES

39 Charles Street London EC1 8BQ

© Macmillan Publishers Limited 1995.

In answer to your letter Worksheet 27

ACTIVITY
Pairwork: writing

AIM
To answer an letter of enquiry about a product.

GRAMMAR AND FUNCTIONS
Can for ability
Writing business letters: *I look forward to..., Could you
please..., Yours faithfully*

VOCABULARY
General: *to serve, to hold (ie contain), to accept, a coin,
change (ie money), memory, to fit, to lock, installation,
a guarantee*

PREPARATION
Make one copy of the worksheet for each pair of students in
the class. Cut out the Student A and Student B sections as
indicated at the top of the worksheet.

TIME
35 minutes

PROCEDURE
1   Tell the students that they are going to write a business
    letter to each other. Discuss some of the conventions of
    letter writing by eliciting phrases for beginning and ending
    letters (*Dear Sir/Madam, Thank you for your letter/recent
    enquiry, I look forward to hearing from you*, etc).

2   Divide the students into two groups of Student As and
    Student Bs and ask them to work with a partner from the
    same group. Give each student the appropriate part of the
    worksheet.

3   In their pairs, ask them to complete the missing words or
    phrases in the letters at the top of the worksheet –
    sometimes one word is necessary, sometimes two or three.
    Although the students are working in pairs, they must both
    complete the missing information. Don't check the letters
    at this stage.

4   When they have done this, ask the students to detach the
    completed letter from the rest of the worksheet and 'send'
    it to a student from the other group. (ie Student A sends to
    Student B, and Student B sends to Student A).

5   Each student now reads the letter they have received and
    then writes an answer to it, using the information they have
    about the product. They should write the reply on the
    headed notepaper at the bottom of the worksheet.

6   When they have finished, ask them to send the reply back
    to the student who wrote the original letter.

7   Ask two or three students to read the letters they have
    received to the rest of the class. Check the completed
    enquiry letters by writing them on the board.

FOLLOW-UP
Ask the students to write a letter enquiring about, or giving
information about, a product they know well.

SUGGESTED ANSWERS

John Coral and Partners
38 Marlborough Road
Swindon SW10 3PT

CCO Vending Machines
39 Charles Street
LONDON EC1 8BQ
12 March 1995

Dear Sir/Madam

I read your advertisement in *The Times* newspaper yesterday and I
would like to have some more information about your vending
machines.

We have had our present machine for four years and need to
replace it. Could you inform me about the price and the
specifications of your ZX190?

I look forward to hearing from you.

Yours faithfully

Jefferson Sanders and Co. Chartered Accountants
78 Grays Road
LONDON N1 4PJ

12 March 1995
Rexa Window Locks
Unit 3B
Wilton Industrial Park
Swindon SW3 6AF

Dear Sir/Madam

We have had some problems with security in our
offices recently. It is an old building which has
many large wooden windows. We are looking for some
good window locks and a colleague recommended your
company to me. Please send me details of your product
range and tell me if you have anything suitable for
us.
I look forward to hearing from you.

Yours faithfully

© Macmillan Publishers Limited 1995.

 Advertising and Trading Standards	You can	You can't
Advertise tobacco		
Compare your product directly with another		
Say things that you cannot prove are true		
Use shocking images in advertisements		
Sell something for more than it says on the label		
Sell food without saying what is in it		
Use artificial colours in food		
Sell a product or service without first telling the customer what he or she will have to pay for it		
Refuse to give the customer his/her money back for a product which doesn't work		
Other _____ _____ _____ _____		

© Macmillan Publishers Limited 1995.

PHOTOCOPIABLE

What are the rules? **Worksheet** *28*

ACTIVITY
Pairwork: speaking

AIM
To talk about advertising and trading standards in different countries.

GRAMMAR AND FUNCTIONS
Can and *can't* for permission and prohibition

VOCABULARY
Trading: *a service, to pay for, to refuse, to give money back, a label, to prove, to compare, to work* (function properly)

PREPARATION
Make one copy of the worksheet for each student in the class.

TIME
30 minutes

PROCEDURE
1 Write the following words on the board and check their meaning and pronunciation, marking the stress where necessary: *image, advertisement, advertise, prove, label, artificial.*

2 Give one worksheet to each student. Ask them to think for a few minutes about advertising rules and practices in their country. They should then read the statements and tick the relevant box on the grid according to the rules in their own country.

3 Ask students to work in pairs or groups of three and discuss their answers.

4 Go through the answers with the whole class, asking them to comment on any practices that they found interesting or surprising.

FOLLOW-UP
Ask students to write a brief description of some of the standards which their company has set itself to ensure good working practice. For example:

A bank:
You can't offer credit without a guarantee.
Customers can keep their personal details secret from the bank.

© Macmillan Publishers Limited 1995.

Reward Pre-intermediate
Business Resource Pack

CHAIRING A MEETING

	You should	You shouldn't
Before the meeting		
At the beginning of the meeting		
During the meeting		
At the end of the meeting		
After the meeting		

GIVING A PRESENTATION

	You should	You shouldn't
Before the presentation		
At the beginning of the presentation		
During the presentation		
At the end of the presentation		

WRITING A REPORT

	You should	You shouldn't
At the beginning of the report		
In the main part of the report		
At the end of the report		

© Macmillan Publishers Limited 1995.

ACTIVITY
Groupwork: speaking

AIM
To discuss techniques for giving a presentation, chairing a meeting and writing a report.

GRAMMAR AND FUNCTIONS
Should and *shouldn't* for advice and recommendations

VOCABULARY
Time expressions: *before, during, after, at the beginning/end*
Communication skills: *to give the background, to interrupt, to introduce, to state one's aims, to summarise, to conclude, to involve (people), to control, to emphasise, to circulate (information), to take notes, to deal with (questions), to divide... into, to give an overview, clear, precise, brief*

PREPARATION
Make one copy of the worksheet for each student in the class.

TIME
30 minutes

PROCEDURE
1 Ask the students whether they have to give presentations, take part in meetings or write reports, and discuss what they like and don't like about these activities.

2 Give each student a copy of the worksheet and ask them to work in groups of three or four to complete the grid. **Do not pre-teach the vocabulary,** but go round supplying the words as you see the need arising and encourage them to use dictionaries.

3 Ask each group to present their ideas to the rest of the class for discussion and comment. This is also the moment to write up the new vocabulary on the board.

FOLLOW-UP
Ask the students to prepare and give a short presentation (about three minutes) on some aspect of their country or company using some of the recommended techniques. The phrases below form a useful reference sheet for these presentations.

Useful phrases for presentations

Opening
I'd like to talk about …
I'm going to tell you a little about…
I'd like to divide my presentation into three parts:
First, …
Secondly, …
Finally, …
I'd like to concentrate on, …

Giving the background
As you (probably) know, …
In the past two years, …

Referring to charts
As you can see from this diagram, …
This chart shows the, …
If you look at this graph, you will see that, …

Moving on
Next, I'd like to discuss…
Now let's move on to the…
Now let's focus on…

Giving examples
An example of this is, …
such as, …

Concluding
Finally, I'd like to say that…
To sum up, …
Thank you for listening. If you have any questions, I'll be happy to answer them.

© Macmillan Publishers Limited 1995.

© Macmillan Publishers Limited 1995.

PHOTOCOPIABLE

Everyday requests **Worksheets**  **30a** and **30b**

NOTE: Use Worksheets 30a and 30b for this activity.

ACTIVITY
Groupwork: speaking

AIM
To make everyday requests when travelling on business.

GRAMMAR AND FUNCTIONS
Requests and asking for permission: *Can/could I/you... ?*
I wonder if you could ...? Do you mind if...? Would you
mind... -ing?

VOCABULARY
Travel: *to change (a flight, some money), to confirm*
an appointment, to lend/borrow something, to reserve
(a table), to recommend, to watch, to have a look at,
a trolley

PREPARATION
Make one copy of Worksheet 30a (board game) and one copy
of Worksheet 30b (cards) for each group of three students. Cut
out the cards and counters as indicated. You will need one
dice for each group. Optional: make one copy of the rules on
the back of Worksheet 30b for each group of three students.

TIME
30 minutes

PROCEDURE
1 Elicit from the students the kind of requests that they might
have to make while on a business trip.
For example: *at the airport, at the hotel* etc.
Write their suggestions on the board.

2 Tell the students that they are going to play a board game
imagining that they are on a business trip in Hong Kong.
Explain that they will need to make various requests for
things in different situations.
For example:
> You want to wake up at seven tomorrow.
> > *Could I have a morning call at seven o'clock,*
> > *please?*
> You want to book an alarm call.
> > *May I have an alarm call for tomorrow morning?*

3 Ask the students to work in groups of three and give each
group a board, a set of cards and counters.

4 Each student chooses a counter. Place the cards face down
in a pile in the middle of the table.

5 Tell the students that each card has a letter on it that
explains where the situation is taking place. The letters
stand for:
> H = hotel
> R = restaurant
> A = airport
> O = office
> T = telephone
> C = conference

6 Explain the rules of the game. (If you like, make one copy
of the rules for each group and give them out or put them
on an OHP.)

FOLLOW-UP
Students write a letter to the Chamber of Commerce in London
requesting information about Business English exams for
learners of English.

© Macmillan Publishers Limited 1995.

Cards

H You arrive at the hotel. What do you say at reception?
Hello. Could I have a single room for two nights?

H You want a newspaper with your breakfast.
Telephone room service.
Could you bring me a newspaper with my breakfast?

H You want to answer any telephone calls in your room.
Ask at hotel reception.
Could you please put my calls through to my room?

H You are ready to leave the hotel and you want to pay. Talk to the hotel receptionist.
Can I have my bill now, please?

R You don't know what is the best thing to eat. Ask your host/hostess.
Can you recommend something?

R You are in a Chinese restaurant. Ask your host/hostess how you use chopsticks.
Could you show me how to use chopsticks?

R You want to eat again at the restaurant at the same time next week. Ask.
Could you reserve a table for me for next week?

A You have no Hong Kong dollars, only US dollars. Ask at the bureau de change.
Could you change these US dollars for me?

A Your flight home is on Tuesday, but you want to leave on Friday. Ask at the booking desk.
Can I change my flight, please?

A You want to go to the city centre. You stop a taxi and speak to the driver.
Can you take me to the city centre, please?

A You are carrying a lot of luggage and want someone to hold the door open for you. Ask a stranger.
Would you mind holding the door open for me?

O You want to send a fax to your company urgently. Ask a secretary.
Can you send this to my company for me, please?

O You have written a 3-page report, but do not have time to type it. Ask a secretary.
Would you mind typing this report for me?

O You want to use the telephone to make an international call. Ask.
Do you mind if I use the phone to make an international call?

O You need a car to visit a client outside the city. Ask a colleague for hers.
Could I borrow your car, please?

T You have a meeting with a client at 11 o'clock, but you will not be free until 12 o'clock. Telephone and ask to change the time.
Could we meet at 12 o'clock?

T You telephone a client to tell her that you have arrived in Hong Kong but she is not there.
Leave a message.
Could you tell her that I've arrived?

T You have a meeting with a client but you are not sure what time. Telephone his secretary.
Could you please confirm the time of our meeting?

C You have lost your conference programme. Ask to see another delegate's.
Could I have a look at your programme?

C You cannot find Room 211. Ask someone the way.
Can you tell me the way to Room 211, please?

C You are sitting at the back of the room and cannot hear what the speaker is saying.
Would you mind speaking a little louder?

© Macmillan Publishers Limited 1995.

Everyday requests **Worksheet** *30b*

HOW TO PLAY THE GAME

1 Player 1 throws the dice and moves his/her counter forward on the board.

2 If he/she lands on a white square, it is then the next player's turn to throw the dice.

3 If he/she lands on a shaded square, the player to his/her right (Player 2) must take a card from the top of the pile. Player 2 must tell Player 1 the letter which is written in the top corner of the card ie: H, T, L etc to explain where the situation is taking place. Player 2 then reads the situation described on the card to Player 1 (but not the answer, of course!).

4 Player 1 must then form an acceptable request to make in this situation. Player 3 should judge whether the request has been phrased correctly and is appropriate. (It doesn't have to be the exact wording on the card, but it must be an appropriate request.) If the request is correct, Player 2 should respond positively to it. If the request is incorrect, Player 1 must go back 3 spaces.

5 It is now Player 2's turn.

6 The game ends when one player reaches the finish.

© Macmillan Publishers Limited 1995.

26-30 | *Business terms*

high	important	quick	serious	main	sharp	up-to-date
temporary	expensive	hard	competitive	useful	low	big

_____ price

_____ decision

_____ competitor

_____ information

_____ meeting

_____ market

_____ worker

_____ equipment

_____ problem

_____ product

_____ increase

- - - - fold -

	You	**Your partner**
Do you like taking quick decisions?		
Who is your company's (or a company you know well) main competitor?		
How does a company obtain up-to-date information about the market?		
How do you prepare for an important meeting?		
Can you give an example of a very competitive market?		
Do you consider yourself to be a hard worker?		
What expensive equipment does your company use?		
What are the main problems for someone starting a new business?		
What are your company's (or a company you know well) main products?		

© Macmillan Publishers Limited 1995.

PHOTOCOPIABLE

Business terms   Worksheet Progress check   26-30

ACTIVITY
Pairwork: speaking

AIM
To familiarise students with adjective-noun collocations commonly used in business.

VOCABULARY
General: *decision, up-to-date, sharp, competitive*

PREPARATION
Make one copy of the worksheet for each student in the class, and fold the worksheet as indicated.

TIME
30 minutes

PROCEDURE

1 Write the word *price* on the board and ask the students to suggest adjectives which could go with it. You are looking for *high, low, competitive, good*, but accept any reasonable answer (**not** *expensive* or *cheap*).

2 Give one worksheet – **folded** so that they cannot see the questions at the bottom – to each student and ask them to work in pairs to find as many adjective-noun combinations as possible for each noun on the list. Ask students to write in the possible adjectives in the space provided next to each noun.

3 Go through the answers with the whole class.

4 Ask the students to unfold their worksheets and read the questions. Ask the students to work alone to complete the section marked 'you'.

5 When they have done this, ask the students to work in pairs and ask and answer the questions with their partner. They should fill in the information in the section marked 'your partner' as they do so.

6 Discuss the answers with the whole class. Is there anything they found particularly interesting or surprising?

FOLLOW-UP
Students choose three or four collocations and make their own sentences or questions to present to the others.

SUGGESTED ANSWERS

high, low	price	*temporary, hard*	worker
quick, important, hard	decision	*expensive, useful, up-to-date*	equipment
main, serious	competitor	*big, serious, main*	problem
up-to-date, useful, important	information	*competitive, main, expensive*	product
useful, important	meeting	*big, sharp*	increase
competitive, important, big	market		

© Macmillan Publishers Limited 1995.

VANESSA SAGE

I first began to feel pains in my hands when I was working in a travel agent's. Every day I had to work on the computer, booking holidays for customers. I was typing about five or six hours a day. One day I was typing a customer's details when I felt a sharp pain. Over the next few weeks the problem got worse and in the end I couldn't move my left hand. Now I can't use a typewriter or computer any more.

TOMAS CZARNECKA

We were working on the construction of a new hospital, installing the electricity supply. When you have worked with electricity for as many years as I have, you don't take any risks and I thought I knew what I was doing. But on this occasion, it was a very hot day and I wasn't wearing my safety gloves. A young engineer who was working on another part of the building switched on the power while I was connecting a cable. I'm lucky to be alive.

BILLY BRAITHWAITE

I remember the day very well. It was three weeks before Christmas. The warehouse was filled with thousands of toys waiting to be delivered to shops all over the country. Every day new toys were arriving and we didn't know where to put them. Inside it was impossible to move. One day I was moving two bicycles, when two heavy boxes fell on me.

MAKIKO KITA

Six months ago they sold our company to a larger group. My boss, who is the managing director, immediately became more involved in the group's activities and less in our company's business. He was spending three or four days a week away from the office. As a result I had more work to do and greater responsibility. I was staying at the office until 9 or 10 in the evening and often at weekends too. Three weeks ago I was talking to a customer on the phone when suddenly I lost consciousness – for about thirty seconds I didn't know where I was. I thought it was strange because I wasn't feeling particularly tired or ill at the time.

	TYPE OF JOB	DESCRIPTION OF ACCIDENT/PROBLEM	REASONS FOR ACCIDENT/PROBLEM	RECOMMENDATIONS
1				
2				
3				
4				

© Macmillan Publishers Limited 1995.

PHOTOCOPIABLE

Health and safety Worksheet **31**

ACTIVITY
Groupwork: reading, speaking

AIM
To describe an accident in the past and talk about its causes.

GRAMMAR AND FUNCTIONS
Past continuous and past simple to describe actions leading up to an event in the past.
Should for recommendations

VOCABULARY
Health: *a pain, safety gloves, to lose consciousness, to be alive, ill, a risk*
General: *to search for, to get worse, to install, to involve, to spend time*

PREPARATION
Make one copy of the table for each student in the class. Cut out the four sections as indicated for each group of two to four students in the class. Each student should have a description of a different accident or problem.

TIME
30 minutes

PROCEDURE
1 Introduce the subject of safety at work by asking students what kind of health risks there are in different places of work such as a factory, an office, a building site etc.

2 Explain that they are going to read about an accident or a problem at work and the events leading up to it.

3 Give each student the table and one of the descriptions.

4 Ask students to read their description and to complete the table. They should not yet fill in the 'Recommendations' section.

5 Ask the students to work in groups of two, three or four to find out about the other accidents or problems from other students in their group. Elicit the questions the students will need to ask.
For example:
What happened to Vanessa?
How did that happen?
What was she doing at the time?

6 Tell the students to fill in the details on the table as they find out the information.

7 When they have finished, ask students to discuss in their groups how this kind of accident/problem can be avoided.
For example:
You should always follow safety procedures.
Ask students to note down their ideas under 'Recommendations'.

8 When they have done this, go through the recommendations with the whole class.

FOLLOW-UP
Ask the students to write a description of an accident or a problem they know about or have experienced. They should ask the group to comment and to make recommendations.

ANSWERS

	TYPE OF JOB	DESCRIPTION OF ACCIDENT/PROBLEM	REASONS FOR ACCIDENT/PROBLEM
1	Typist	sharp pain in hand	typing for 5-6 hours a day
2	Electrical engineer	nearly electrocuted	not wearing safety gloves
3	Storeman	hit by two heavy boxes	overcrowded warehouse; boxes piled too high
4	Secretary	lost consciousness	stress due to overwork

© Macmillan Publishers Limited 1995.

A When did it happen and why?

■ Levi Strauss made the first jeans

■ On 'Black Monday' share prices on Wall Street fell over 20% in one day.

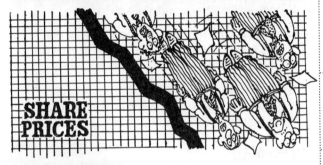

■ At the Earth Summit in Rio world leaders agreed to do more to protect the environment.

■ The 'Rectigraph' (or photocopier, as it is now known) was patented in America.

B

In 1850 during the Gold Rush thousands of miners were arriving in San Francisco to look for gold.

Strauss was selling denim cloth for making tents.

A miner complained that his trousers were not strong enough for his work.

On stock markets around the world dealers were using computers to control trading.

The US government was borrowing large amounts of money from foreign investors.

In 1987 US interest rates suddenly began to rise.

Scientists were becoming more and more worried about pollution, particularly from developing countries.

The Green movement was growing in the West.

By 1992 governments realised that they had to take action.

In 1903 the US government was selling land in Oklahoma to thousands of families.

George Beidler was copying contracts by hand for new land owners.

Beidler had the idea of using a camera.

© Macmillan Publishers Limited 1995.

PHOTOCOPIABLE

The conditions for change Worksheet 32

ACTIVITY
Groupwork: reading, speaking

AIM
To speak about the background to important events.

GRAMMAR AND FUNCTIONS
Past continuous for describing background events

VOCABULARY
General: *to protect, to patent, to copy, to take action, a miner, a contract, an investor, a tent, a developing country*

PREPARATION
Make one copy of the section marked A of the worksheet for each student in the class and one copy of the section marked B for each group of two to four students. Cut out the sentences as indicated.

TIME
30 minutes

PROCEDURE
1 Write the following sentence on the board.
The Berlin Wall came down.
Ask the students to say when this happened (1989) and what was happening in the world at the time.
For example:
In Eastern Europe Communist governments were falling.

2 Tell the students they are going to try and put a date to other events and describe what was happening in the world at that time.

3 Divide the class into groups of up to four students. Give each student a copy of the section marked A of the worksheet with the four main events and ask them to discuss a) when each one happened and b) why it happened (ie what was happening at the time).

4 Go through the answers with the whole class.

5 Give each group a set of the sentences in the section marked B, cut out and jumbled up. Ask them to find three events which led up to each of the four main events.

6 When they have finished, ask them to put away the sentences. Then ask a student from each group to describe the background situation to one of the four main events.

FOLLOW-UP
Ask the students to prepare another such story to present in the next lesson. It could be the story (real or imaginary) of a scientific breakthrough, an economic disaster, or a technical development.

ANSWERS

Levi Strauss
In 1850 during the Gold Rush thousands of miners were arriving in San Francisco to look for gold.
Strauss was selling denim cloth for making tents.
A miner complained that his trousers were not strong enough for his work.

Black Monday
On stock markets around the world dealers were using computers to control trading.
The US government was borrowing large amounts of money from foreign investors.
In 1987 US interest rates suddenly began to rise.

The Earth Summit
Scientists were becoming more and more worried about pollution, particularly from developing countries.
The Green movement was growing in the West.
By 1992 governments realised that they had to take action.

The 'Rectigraph'
In 1903 the US government was selling land in Oklahoma to thousands of families.
George Beidler was copying contracts by hand for new land owners.
Beidler had the idea of using a camera.

© Macmillan Publishers Limited 1995.

Student A

Read the fax.

FRAISJUS 4100 COMPIEGNE FRANCE

Attention: Vidal Garcia, Purchasing Department

Fax: 34 6 588 310

From: Jean-Luc Matthias, Sales Manager

Dear Sr Garcia,

Thank you for your order of 2000 cartons of pineapple juice. They will be ready for collection next Tuesday. Please can you collect them from our warehouse on that day at 8.00 a.m.

Yours sincerely

Jean-Luc Matthias

Write the reply.

- not company policy to collect goods

- insurance and transport too expensive

- supplier must deliver goods to Mercanda warehouse in Zaragoza

MERCANDA SUPERMARKETS

16001 Valencia

Attention: Jean-Luc Matthias

Fax: 33 1 44 88 97 94

From: Vidal Garcia, Purchasing Department

Dear M Matthias,

Thank you for your fax.

I look forward to hearing from you.

Yours sincerely

Vidal Garcia

Student B

Read the fax.

FRAISJUS 4100 COMPIEGNE FRANCE

Attention: Vidal Garcia, Purchasing Department

Fax: 34 6 588 310

From: Jean-Luc Matthias, Sales Manager

Dear Sr Garcia

I am sorry to inform you that the batch of 2000 cartons of pineapple juice left our plant 24 hours late and will not arrive until Wednesday.

Please accept my apologies.

Yours sincerely

Jean-Luc Matthias

Write the reply.

- last batch arrived late

- juice bad: temperature in lorry too high

- we expect your insurance to pay

MERCANDA SUPERMARKETS

16001 Valencia

Attention: Jean-Luc Matthias

Fax: 33 1 44 88 97 94

From: Vidal Garcia, Purchasing Department

Dear M Matthias,

I am writing concerning…

I look forward to hearing from you.

Yours sincerely

Vidal Garcia

© Macmillan Publishers Limited 1995.

A problem with a supplier

ACTIVITY
Pairwork: reading, writing faxes

AIM
To take part in a typical exchange of faxes between a large customer and supplier.

GRAMMAR AND FUNCTIONS
Too + adjective; *not* + adjective + *enough*

VOCABULARY
Trade: *to order, to collect, to deliver, a sample, a batch, goods, transport, insurance*
Faxes: *look forward to hearing, concerning, to inform*

PREPARATION
Make a copy of the worksheet for each student in the class. Cut out the Student A and Student B sections as indicated.

TIME
30 minutes

PROCEDURE
1 Tell the students that they work in the purchasing department of Mercanda Supermarkets, a large supermarket chain, and are going to deal with some faxes from a supplier.

2 Divide the class into two groups of Student As and Student Bs and ask the students to work with a partner from the same group. Give each student the appropriate part of the worksheet.

3 Ask the students to read the faxes from the supplier, Fraisjus.

4 When they are ready, ask them to work with their partner to write suitable replies using the notes provided.

5 When the students have finished, put them into new pairs of one Student A and one Student B to compare their faxes.

6 Ask one or two of the students to read their replies to the class.

FOLLOW-UP
Playing the role of the supplier, students choose one of the faxes they have written and reply to it.

ANSWERS

MERCANDA SUPERMARKETS

16001 Valencia

Attention: Jean-Luc Matthias

Fax: 33 1 44 88 97 94

From: Vidal Garcia, Purchasing Department

Dear M Matthias,

Thank you for your fax, which I received this morning. I am afraid it is not our policy to collect goods from the supplier. The cost of insurance and transport is too high. Please can you deliver the goods to our main warehouse in Zaragoza.

I look forward to hearing from you.

Yours sincerely

Vidal Garcia

MERCANDA SUPERMARKETS

16001 Valencia

Attention: Jean-Luc Matthias

Fax: 33 1 44 88 97 94

From: Vidal Garcia, Purchasing Department

Dear M Matthias,

I am writing concerning the last batch of pineapple juice that we received. Firstly, it arrived late.
Secondly, the temperature in the container lorry was too high and the juice was bad. We will, of course, expect your insurance to pay.

I look forward to hearing from you.

Yours sincerely

Vidal Garcia

© Macmillan Publishers Limited 1995.

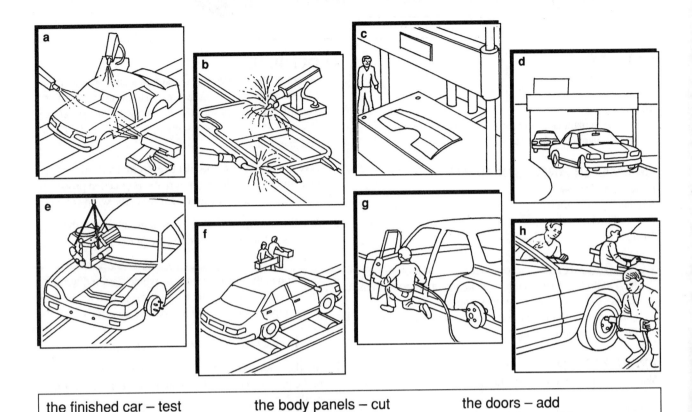

the finished car – test	the body panels – cut	the doors – add
the car – despatch	the components – fit	the panels – weld
the body – paint	the engine – put in	

Notes
Building A is old and too low for the pressing machines.
The cutting and pressing machines are very noisy.
The assembly line needs a lot of space.
The paintshop must be in a clean and separate building.
There mustn't be too much noise near the hospital.
The stores must be near the main road.

Choose a suitable building to locate each of the following.

the paintshop   the welding area   quality control & testing

the assembly line   the stores   the press shop

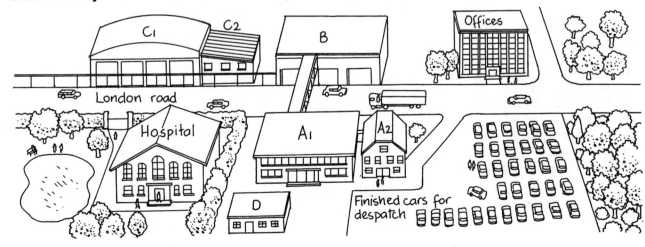

© Macmillan Publishers Limited 1995.

PHOTOCOPIABLE

A manufacturing process   Worksheet

ACTIVITY
Groupwork: speaking

AIM
To describe a manufacturing process and decide on the layout of a manufacturing plant.

GRAMMAR AND FUNCTIONS
Present simple passive
Sequencing: *first, then*
Too + adjective
Must

VOCABULARY
Production: *to test, to despatch, to weld, to cut, to press, to fit, to add, to paint, a panel, supplies, finished product, a component, an assembly line, a paintshop, a press shop, the stores, quality control*

PREPARATION
Make one copy of the worksheet for each student in the class.

TIME
30 minutes

PROCEDURE
1   Introduce the subject of manufacturing and ask students to name the different stages in a manufacturing process. For example: *delivery of supplies, assembly, testing, packing, despatch.* Elicit adverbs of sequence: *first, secondly, then, next, after that, finally.*

2   Give a copy of the worksheet to each student and focus their attention on the pictures of the production process of a car manufacturing plant, which are in the wrong order.

3   Ask the students to work in pairs or groups to put the pictures in the right order using the phrases below to help them.

4   Go through the answers with the whole class and write them on the board. Encourage students to turn the phrases into complete sentences with a passive construction. For example:
    First the body panels are cut. Then…

5   Ask the students to study the diagram showing the layout of the plant and to read the sentences under the section marked 'Notes'.

6   Ask the students to look at the list of different sites listed at the bottom of the worksheet. Explain that they must choose a suitable location for each stage of the process.

7   Ask students to work in pairs or groups to decide which location on the diagram is best suited for each function, bearing in mind the sentences under the 'Notes' section.

8   When they have finished, ask the students to present their layout to the rest of the class and to give reasons for their decisions.

FOLLOW-UP
Ask the students to work in pairs to draw their own plan of the layout of a factory and then to take another pair of students on a guided tour of the plant, explaining the various steps in the process as they go.

ANSWERS

a   the body panels are cut.
b   the panels are welded.
c   the body is painted.
d   the components are fitted.
e   the doors are added.
f   the engine is put in.
g   the finished car is tested.
h   the car is despatched.

© Macmillan Publishers Limited 1995.

STUDENT A

MENU
· · ·
Starters
SMOKED MACKEREL PATÉ
(A light paté made of fish and butter, served with lemon.)

· · ·
Main courses
OXFORD PIE
(Pieces of steak in a dark sauce made with beer, cooked with mushrooms and with pastry on top.)

· · ·
Desserts
BAKED APPLES
(Whole apples cooked slowly in the oven with raisins and brown sugar.)

Service is not included in the bill.

STUDENT B

MENU
♦ ♦ ♦
Starters
GAME SOUP
(A rich soup made from different types of game.)

♦ ♦ ♦
Main courses
SALT BEEF & DUMPLINGS
(Beef boiled in salted water with carrots, onions and balls of bread.)

♦ ♦ ♦
Desserts
SIMNEL CAKE
(A rich heavy fruit cake made with almonds and honey.)

Service is not included in the bill.

© Macmillan Publishers Limited 1995.

Entertaining a client   Worksheet   35

ACTIVITY
Pairwork: speaking

AIM
To explain the dishes on a menu to a guest and make recommendations.

GRAMMAR AND FUNCTIONS
Revision of present simple passive

Suggestions and recommendations: *I recommend… You really should try…*

VOCABULARY
Food and cooking: *to bake, to grill, to fry, to boil, to roast, a local speciality, a traditional dish*

Taste: *sweet, salty, bitter, spicy, rich, hot, mild, filling, light, heavy*

PREPARATION
Make one copy of the worksheet for each pair of students in the class. Cut out the Student A and Student B sections as indicated.

TIME
30 minutes

PROCEDURE

1 Write a menu similar to the one on the worksheet on the board and write in one starter, one main course and one dessert.

2 Set the scene. Tell the students that you are in a restaurant in Britain and the students are your guests. Elicit questions about what is on the menu.
For example:
   Student: *What is trifle?*
   You: *A very sweet traditional English pudding.*
   Student: *What is it made of?*
   You: *Fruit, cream and sponge.*
   Student: *Do you recommend it?*
   You: *Yes, definitely.*

3 Ask the students to imagine that they have taken a client to a restaurant.

4 Divide the class equally into Student As and Student Bs. Give each student a copy of the appropriate menu. Ask them to write in two more dishes under each heading on their menu. They should choose specialities from their region or dishes that are unlikely to be known to their partner.

5 Ask the students to work in pairs of one Student A and one Student B and to exchange menus.

6 When they have studied their partner's menu, they should ask each other about the various dishes, taking turns to play the roles of host and guest. Go round and listen to the conversations, supplying any vocabulary when needed.

FOLLOW-UP
Write a letter to a business contact thanking him/her for entertaining you one evening last week.

© Macmillan Publishers Limited 1995.

31-35 | *Phrasal verbs*

_____ a successful conference

_____ a visitor

_____ employees

_____ a new market

_____ someone's address

_____ a company

_____ a difficult decision

_____ time and money

_____ a difficult period

find out	**go through**	**look up**	**take on**	**lay off**	**break into**	**run out of**
look after	**set up**	**put off**	**look forward to**	**take over**		

✂

Yes it's a very competitive market.	Yes, thirty people lost their jobs.	Yes, it's going to be an interesting trip.
Was it difficult to break into the Japanese market?	Did the company lay off any staff?	Are you looking forward to your visit to the Far East?
Yes, I must order some more from the printers.	Yes, they told me it leaves at 2 o'clock.	Yes, but she wasn't in the phone book.
Have we run out of brochures?	Did you find out what time the train leaves?	Did you look up her phone number?
Yes, we are owned by Needmans now.	Yes, everyone was very kind and helpful.	Yes, but things are much easier now.
Has your company been taken over?	Did they look after you well?	Did you go through a difficult period?
Yes, she's going to start work next week.	Well, OK but I really must see you before the end of the week.	Yes, she was tired of working for other people.
Have you taken on a new assistant?	Can we put off our meeting today?	Has she set up her own company?

© Macmillan Publishers Limited 1995.

PHOTOCOPIABLE

Phrasal verbs   Worksheet Progress check   31–35

ACTIVITY

Pairwork or groupwork: speaking

NB: The game can be played as a card game for two or more
players (see below for instructions).

AIM

To be familiar with the meaning and use of some phrasal verbs
commonly used in business.

GRAMMAR AND FUNCTIONS

Revision of *Yes/No* questions
Mixed tenses

VOCABULARY

Phrasal verbs: *look forward to, look after, take on/lay off,
break into, find out/look up, take over/set up, put off,
run out of, go through*

PREPARATION

Make one copy of the top half of the worksheet for each
student. Make one copy of the bottom half (the cards) for each
group of three to four students.

TIME

30 minutes

PROCEDURE

1   Introduce the idea of phrasal verbs by writing the phrases
below on the board and eliciting the phrasal verb
equivalents in brackets.
   continue talking (go on)
   stop smoking (give up)
   calculate prices (work out)

2   Give a copy of the top half of the worksheet to each
student and ask them to look at the phrasal verbs in
the box.

3   Ask students to work in pairs to match the phrasal verbs in
the box to the words or phrases above. Tell them that
some phrasal verbs can go with more than one word or
phrase.

4   Go through the answers with the whole class.

Answers
look forward to a successful conference
look after a visitor
take on/lay off employees
break into a new market
look up/find out someone's address
take over/set up a company
put off a difficult decision
run out of time and money
go through a difficult period

5   Ask the students to work in small groups. Distribute one set
of cards evenly between the players in each group.

6   Give students a copy of the instructions 'How to play', or
put them on an OHP. Go through the rules and check they
understand.

7   The students are now ready to play the game.

FOLLOW-UP

Ask the students to write illustrative sentences of their own
using the phrasal verbs in the box.

PAIRWORK OPTION

Alternative game for pairs of students:
1   Each pair needs a complete set of cards.
2   Each pair puts all the cards face down in a pile.
3   In turns, each student takes a card and (without showing
the card) reads the answer to the other player to elicit the
question (as in 2 and 3 below).
4   A correct question means that the player keeps the card;
otherwise it is returned to the bottom of the pile.
5   The winner is the player with the most cards at the end of
the game.

HOW TO PLAY

The aim is to 'cross off' all the phrasal verbs in the box on the
worksheet.
1   First, students look at the cards in their hand. They cross off
the list on the worksheet any phrasal verbs that also appear
on their cards .
2   Students then take it in turns to read the **answer** at the top
of each of their cards.
3   The other students must then form a **question** (using one of
the phrasal verbs on the list) that would elicit the answer
that has just been read to them.
   For example:

   Student l: *Yes, it's a very competitive market.*
   Student 2: *Was it difficult to **break into** the Japanese
   market?*

4   If a student forms a correct question (though not necessarily
the same as the one on the card), they can cross the phrasal
verb they have used off their list. If they do not form an
appropriate question they cannot cross it off their list. It is
now the next player's turn to read the answer on their card.
5   The winner is the student who is the first to cross off all the
phrasal verbs from the box.

© Macmillan Publishers Limited 1995.

JAPANESE COMPANIES WELCOME HERE SAYS PRIME MINISTER

ENGINEER'S REPORT SAYS TUNNEL IS UNSAFE

KNOX OIL & GAS INCREASES ITS SHAREHOLDING IN BURMAH

WORRIES AS ITALIAN LIRA FALLS AGAIN ON FOREIGN EXCHANGE MARKETS

TOIDA MOTOR COMPANY ANNOUNCES SHARP DROP IN DEMAND FOR NEW CARS

IBERIA INDUSTRIAL GROUP SAY LABOUR COSTS IN SPAIN ARE TOO HIGH

RAILWAY UNION SAYS 2% PAY RISE IS NOT ENOUGH

COURT HEARS HOW AIRLINE 'STOLE' CUSTOMERS FROM OTHER AIRLINES

ESPINOSA FAMILY UNABLE TO AGREE ABOUT FUTURE OF COMPANY

© Macmillan Publishers Limited 1995.

PHOTOCOPIABLE

Business news   Worksheet

ACTIVITY
Pairwork: speaking, reading

AIM
To read items of business news and discuss their implications.

GRAMMAR AND FUNCTIONS
Might for future possibility
Speculating about the future: *might/may, will, probably*

VOCABULARY
Business news: to *announce, to hear, a shareholding, a pay rise, an airline, labour costs, the foreign exchange markets, to devalue (a currency), to set up, to close, to lay off, to take over, to go on strike, to pay compensation, to move (relocate)*
General: *a court, a tunnel, worry, unsafe*

PREPARATION
Make one copy of the worksheet for each student in the class.

TIME
30 minutes

PROCEDURE
1 Write this headline on the board and ask the students to make it into a full sentence.
> *CAA LOSES BIG EUROPEAN DEFENCE CONTRACT TO US COMPANY*
> *CAA has lost a big European defence contract to an American company.*

2 Ask the students what they think might happen next. For example:
> *CAA might lay off some employees.*
> *Perhaps the government will help CAA with other contracts.*

3 Give one worksheet to each student and ask them to check the meaning of each headline, using a dictionary where necessary. Check the pronunciation of new vocabulary by asking students to read each headline aloud.

4 Ask students to work in pairs to discuss the meaning of each headline and to speculate about what is going to happen next.

5 Discuss the answers with the whole class.

FOLLOW-UP
Ask the students to bring in similar headlines from English newspapers or from papers in their own language. They can explain these to the rest of the class who will then speculate about what will happen next.
Alternatively, ask them to choose one of the headlines on the worksheet and write the accompanying story (50–80 words).

© Macmillan Publishers Limited 1995.

1 **Machine parts manufacturer.** The price of steel (your main material) has just gone up by 3%.
Option 1: Pass on the increase to the customer (put up the price of the finished product).
Option 2: Do not increase the price.

2 **A law firm.** One of the clerks has just retired. He was not a very efficient worker.
Option 1: Replace him with a new member of staff.
Option 2: Give his work to other employees in the department.

3 **A bank.** An important customer is nine months late with payments on a loan.
Option 1: Ask for all the money back immediately.
Option 2: Give the customer longer to pay.

4 **A furniture retailer.** Your warehouse is too full.
Option 1: Reduce your stock.
Option 2: Rent another warehouse.

5 **A hi-fi manufacturer.** A company in Spain has asked if they can make one of your products under licence.
Option 1: Sell them the licence to manufacture the product.
Option 2: Export the product to Spain yourself, using your own agent to sell it.

6 **An insurance company.** Car crime has increased sharply in cities.
Option 1: Put all car insurance premiums up by 3%.
Option 2: Put up the premium for people living in the city by 8%.

7 **A computer software consultant.** A large company has asked you to write an office management system. This will provide enough work for all your staff for 2 years.
Option 1: Share the contract with another company.
Option 2: Take on the whole contract yourself.

© Macmillan Publishers Limited 1995.

Discussing options Worksheet

ACTIVITY
Pairwork or groupwork: speaking

AIM
To discuss the consequences of different courses of action and decide which is best.

GRAMMAR AND FUNCTIONS
First conditional/*should* (for advice)

VOCABULARY
General: *to pass on/to absorb (the cost), to replace (a person), to rent, to make (a product) under licence, to export, to put up (the price), to share, to take on (work), steel, a clerk, an insurance premium, crime*

PREPARATION
Make one copy of the worksheet for each student in the class.

TIME
40 minutes

PROCEDURE

1 Give a worksheet to each student and focus their attention on the first situation.

2 Explain to the students that they are going to look at different situations and decide what they should do, and to think about the consequences of various options.
Model the activity like this:
> *As you know the price of steel has just gone up by 3%. This puts us in a difficult position. We can either pass on the increase to our customers or we can absorb the increase ourselves.*

3 Invite students to say what the company should do, and what the consequences of the different options will be. Write some suggestions on the board, so students have a model of the structure you want them to use.
> *We shouldn't put up the price. If we put up the price the customers will be unhappy.*

Encourage the students to use the first conditional construction in their answers.

4 Ask the students to work in groups of two, three or four to study the other situations and discuss the consequences of the options mentioned on the worksheet.

5 Check the answers with the whole class.

6 Ask students to think of another problem for a company, real or imaginary, to present to the rest of the class in the same way.

FOLLOW-UP
Ask the students to write a short memo to their manager, describing one of the problems already discussed, outlining the options and recommending a particular course of action.

© Macmillan Publishers Limited 1995.

1 YOU INHERIT $500,000.
WOULD YOU…

a) start your own company? If so, what kind of company?
b) continue in your present job and invest the money? If so, what in?
c) do something different? If so, what?

---

2 AS THE MOST SUCCESSFUL NEW EMPLOYEE IN THE COMPANY, YOU ARE OFFERED A 'YEAR OFF'.
WOULD YOU…

a) use the time for training? If so, what would you study?
b) work on a project of your own? If so, what?
c) do something completely different? If so, what?

3 A COLLEAGUE RECEIVES PROMOTION WHEN YOU WERE EXPECTING TO GET THE JOB.
WOULD YOU…

a) talk to her about it? If so, what would you say?
b) talk to your boss about it? If so, what would you say?
c) do something different? If so, what?

---

4 YOU ARE PLANNING A BUSINESS TRIP TO NEW YORK FOR YOURSELF AND FOUR OTHER DIRECTORS.
WOULD YOU…

a) choose only the best transport and accommodation? If so, how would you explain this to the Finance Director?
b) try to keep costs down? If so, what would you say to the other directors?
c) try to do both? If so, how would you travel and where would you stay?

5 A TV DOCUMENTARY SAYS THAT YOUR BRAND OF LEMONADE CAUSES HEADACHES.
WOULD YOU…

a) withdraw the lemonade? If so, what would you tell the public?
b) continue selling the lemonade? If so, what would you tell the public?
c) do something completely different? If so, what?

---

6 SOMEONE IN YOUR DEPARTMENT IS USING THE TELEPHONE TO MAKE EXPENSIVE PERSONAL CALLS. LAST MONTH YOU SENT A MEMO TO EVERYONE ABOUT THE PROBLEM, BUT NOTHING HAS CHANGED.
WOULD YOU…

a) call in the police? If so, would you tell everyone or keep it secret?
b) speak to your staff? If so, what would you say?
c) do something completely different? If so, what?

© Macmillan Publishers Limited 1995.

PHOTOCOPIABLE

What would you do ... ? **Worksheet** 38

ACTIVITY
Groupwork: speaking

AIM
To discuss possible solutions to a problem and to consider the possible consequences.

GRAMMAR AND FUNCTIONS
Second conditional

VOCABULARY
General: *to withdraw (a product), to inherit, to keep (something) secret, a year off, promotion*

PREPARATION
Make one copy of the worksheet for each student in the class.

TIME
30 minutes

PROCEDURE
1 Give one copy of the worksheet to each student and focus their attention on the situations. Check they know the meaning of the new vocabulary.

2 Ask students to work in pairs or small groups to discuss the questions and to say what they would do in the various situations. They should ask each other to give reasons for their views.

3 Go through the answers with the whole class, encouraging students to comment on the decisions taken.

OPTION
1 Put students in pairs or groups.

2 Each student chooses one of the three options and defends the case for it (ie everyone in the group backs a different option).

FOLLOW-UP
Ask the students to think of other, similar situations for discussion and to be prepared to present these to the class and to say what they themselves would do.

© Macmillan Publishers Limited 1995.

You think...

a You're asking for too much.

b Please don't interrupt.

c I must say one thing.

e OK

d We will not supply any goods without payment first.

g I can't make that decision myself.

f First, what we want is this...

h What is there in the deal for us?

But you say...

1 I need to discuss that with my manager. (would) _____ ☐

2 That is very difficult for us. (would) _____ ☐

3 I want to start by explaining our position. (would like) _____ ☐

4 Can I just make one point? (could) _____ ☐

5 Sorry, can I just finish? (could) _____ ☐

6 We expect you to pay in advance. (would) _____ ☐

7 That's fine. (would) _____ ☐

8 What can you offer us in return? (could) _____ ☐

© Macmillan Publishers Limited 1995.

PHOTOCOPIABLE

Diplomacy Worksheet *39*

ACTIVITY
Pairwork: speaking

AIM
To speak diplomatically when negotiating.

GRAMMAR AND FUNCTIONS
Would and *could* for polite requests in negotiations

VOCABULARY
Negotiation: *to offer (something) in return, to pay in advance, to interrupt, to explain one's position, to make a point*

PREPARATION
Make one copy of the worksheet for each student in the class.

TIME
20 minutes

PROCEDURE
1 Introduce the idea of language appropriacy by asking students how they would ask a) a friend and b) the bank to lend them some money.
  For example:
  a) *John. Can you lend me £10 for a taxi?*
  b) *Good morning. Would it be possible to arrange a loan to buy a car?*

2 Tell them that they are going to look at ways of expressing themselves more diplomatically in different situations.

3 Give a worksheet to each student and ask them why the phrases in thought bubbles would not be appropriate in a formal business negotiation (they are too direct).

4 Ask students to work in pairs to match the phrases in the thought bubbles with their spoken equivalent in the sentences under the heading 'But you say...'. Explain that they should put the letter next to the speech bubble in the corresponding sentence box at the bottom of the worksheet.

5 When they have finished, go through the answers with the whole class.

6 Focus the students' attention on the sentences. Ask them to rephrase the sentences, using *would* or *could* to complete the process of making 'correct and diplomatic' sentences. Check the answers with the whole class.

FOLLOW-UP
Ask the students to look at this short informal letter to a colleague and then to write a similar, but more formal letter to a customer.
Dear Diana
I got your note about the coffee cups. If you want some, you'll need to fill out this staff order form. Be quick because the offer of 10 per cent discount only lasts until the end of the month.
Best wishes
Stan

ANSWERS

1g 2a 3f 4c 5b 6d 7e 8 h

But you say ...

1 I would need to discuss that with my manager.

2 That would be very difficult for us.

3 I would like to start by explaining our position.

4 Could I just make one point?

5 Could I finish?

6 Would you pay in advance?

7 That would be fine.

8 What could you offer us in return?

© Macmillan Publishers Limited 1995.

Student A

Your name	Will Hay
Occupation	Managing Director
Company	Spieling Inc, manufacturers of tennis equipment (racquets, balls, shoes, clothes)
History	In the 1970s Spieling was a famous name and 2 world champions used your equipment
Profile	Sales are low and the company badly needs new marketing ideas
Strategy	To persuade the world's newest tennis star to promote your products (eg Magnus Lundstrøm)

NEGOTIATING BRIEF

You can offer

- $2 million over 3 years
- free equipment and good practice facilities
- publicity
- the chance of a career with the company when the player retires

You want

- exclusive rights for 5 years: Magnus must use only Spieling equipment and clothing
- 30 days a year of Magnus' time for promotional work (photographs, exhibition games, interviews and testing of equipment)
- to choose an agent to protect Magnus' 'image' (to manage press interviews and generally to look after him)

Student B

Your name	Magnus Lundstrøm
Age	18 years
Occupation	Tennis player, ranked No. 17 in the world (playing professionally for 18 months)
Interests	Playing tennis; spending time privately. Managing your own business interests

NEGOTIATING BRIEF

You can offer

- excellent publicity (you expect to be one of the top five players in the world next year)
- 1 day a month for photographs, interviews or exhibition games (possibly two days in the winter months)

You want

- good practice facilities
- to continue to use the racquet you use at the moment (a Wilson)
- a percentage of sales (for products which carry your name)
- a two-year contract (not longer)
- some free time to yourself

© Macmillan Publishers Limited 1995.

PHOTOCOPIABLE

Negotiation Worksheet 40

ACTIVITY
Pairwork: speaking

AIM
To arrange a meeting and to negotiate the terms of a contract.

GRAMMAR AND FUNCTIONS
Second conditional: *would* and *could*
Making proposals, accepting and refusing
Arranging a meeting

VOCABULARY
Negotiation: *to persuade, a two-year contract, a percentage of sales, exclusive rights*
Tennis: a racket, a player, to be ranked, a world champion, an exhibition game

PREPARATION
Make one copy of the worksheet for each pair of students in the class. Cut out Student A and Student B sections as indicated.

TIME
40 minutes

PROCEDURE

1 Introduce the subject of tennis and sponsorship by asking the students who the leading tennis champions are at the moment. Ask other questions, like:
How much money do they make a year ?
What do they have to do for it?
Who sponsors their equipment?

2 Tell the students that they are going to take part in a negotiation, but that first they need to arrange a time and place for the meeting.

3 Ask the students to work in pairs and divide them into Student A and Student B. Give each student the appropriate part of the worksheet. Ask students to read the profile at the top of their worksheet.

4 Ask the students to sit back-to-back, one Student A and one Student B. Explain that Student A (Will Hay) is going to telephone Student B (Magnus Lundstrøm) to arrange a time to meet. Student A should also explain what the meeting is about but they should **not** discuss terms at this stage.

5 When they have done this, ask the students to study their negotiating brief for five minutes to prepare for the meeting.

6 Now ask students to sit face to face and, working in the same pairs, to negotiate the contract. Encourage them to keep discussing terms until they have reached an agreement. They can invent other options, not on the worksheet, if they wish.

7 Ask each pair to report back to the whole class on the results of their discussion.

FOLLOW-UP
Ask the students to write a short memo confirming the terms of the agreement which they have just reached.

© Macmillan Publishers Limited 1995.

Progress check

36-40 | *An informal meeting*

Reward Pre-intermediate
Business Resource Pack

You are sales manager for a company which makes bedroom furniture. Reporting to you there is a team of 28 sales representatives. Each one is responsible for a different area and they travel all over Britain and in Europe. You are looking for ways to motivate them to sell more. At the moment 75% of their salary is fixed and 25% is paid in the form of individual commission.

Possible new incentives

- **Smaller fixed salary, more on commission**
- **Team (not individual) commission**
- **Bonus payments**
- **A share in company profits**
- **Competitions and prizes (cash, holidays, etc)**
- **Non-financial incentives such as training, promotion, time off**
- **Other?**

MEMO

To	The Sales Director
From	Sales working committee
Subject	Report on meeting to discuss motivation of sales team
Date	12 December

At a meeting of sales managers last Friday, we decided to recommend the following action to motivate the sales team and to increase sales.

1 _____

_____

2 _____

_____

3 _____

_____

We look forward to receiving your comments on these suggestions.

© Macmillan Publishers Limited 1995.

An informal meeting   Worksheet Progress check   36-40

ACTIVITY
Groupwork: speaking

AIM
To discuss possible ways of motivating a sales team.

GRAMMAR AND FUNCTIONS
First and second conditional

VOCABULARY
Incentives and selling: *to work on commission, to motivate, to reward, an incentive, a bonus, a prize*

PREPARATION
Make one copy of the worksheet for each student in the class.

TIME
25 minutes

PROCEDURE

1   Ask the students how sales representatives are usually paid and how they can be motivated to sell more. Elicit the phrase, *on a commission basis*.

2   Give one worksheet to each student and ask them to read the paragraph at the top of the worksheet. They should then turn over their worksheet and summarise the situation to the student next to them.

3   Ask the students to work alone and read the list under 'Possible new incentives'. Tell them that they should prepare for a meeting with senior colleagues to discuss the problem the company is facing and to suggest some possible incentives.

4   Divide the students into small groups of three to five to discuss the possibilities and agree on the three best incentives.

5   The students should complete the memo at the bottom of the worksheet with their three suggestions.

6   Ask the students to report their decision to the rest of the class, giving reasons for it.

FOLLOW-UP
Ask the students to write a short report summarising what they discussed and decided, using the framework at the bottom of the worksheet.

© Macmillan Publishers Limited 1995.